Tales of Hope:

Life lessons from a missionary to Africa

Written by **Stephen M. DeMoss**

2024
Merry and Blessed Christmas to David.
From Chris and Hope

Dedication

These writings are dedicated to my dearest parents Robert and Dora DeMoss.
Dad taught and inspired me to "Go into all the world and make disciples of every tribe and tongue."
Mom taught me how to lay down my life, and to do it with joy!
Thank you Lord for giving me the eternal gift of two godly parents.

TABLE OF CONTENTS

Preface
Rose Marie Miller

In 1975, when refugees arrived in Philadelphia from Uganda, we never dreamed that granting hospitality to a persecuted pastor and his family would expand into a mission and painting company that would reach 27 countries and care for 300 workers. But this is what happened.

We came to realize that God's relentless pursuit of bringing every tongue, tribe, and nation into his kingdom family is what God was doing. When the refugees arrived, they pleaded with us to pray that Idi Amin, a cruel and evil dictator, would leave the country. Four years later he did. The pastor, whose name was Kefa Sempangi, returned to his homeland to be part of the new government for the rebuilding of a war-ravaged country.

In December of 1979, at Kefa's insistence, we embarked, with four young men, to seek out the homeless whose parents had been killed in the civil strife. We were stunned by the devastation that Amin had left. There was nothing in the stores, and the homeless slept under fruit stalls in the marketplace.

A home for orphans was born from that dire need.

Since there was so much poverty, it was eventually decided to also start a painting company, which would serve the dual purpose of teaching young men a trade while giving them gainful employment, and simultaneously raising money for the mission project. At the same time my husband Jack was busy training leaders to be church elders. From this training a church was formed.

Steve DeMoss was one of those young men who came in the early stages and then persisted through the decades, returning yearly to teach and train, while developing friendships for the kingdom. This pattern of ministry continued throughout the years --- fostering of relationships, evangelism, providing jobs, teaching and training of local church leaders. Steve tells me there are now 88 churches.

What was the driving force of this movement of grace? A passion for the glory of God, for obeying His mandate to go into all the world to seek out the lost and enfold them into God's kingdom of glory. Not every ministry spawned from the original one is identical. But what all have in common is the purpose of bringing glory to God, whether by medical work, by mitigating economic hardship, or by coming alongside existing churches to partner in the gospel.

The training model of church leaders included a two-month summer internship, followed by a two-year apprenticeship. Many who attended decided to commit to Uganda full-time. Jack would often say to new recruits, "Come and die." This literally could have happened to us when soldiers arrived at our door the first year, demanding we open up. They were searching for young men to arrest them. We were hiding one. Jack slowly approached the door, and armed military men were standing there with demands. Jack did not invite them in, but prayed with them. They left.

Prayer is an integral part of our mission. Not only prayer for those we came to serve, but for us who served, since all are needy for grace.

In this book you have in your hands, Steve DeMoss invites all to join the ranks of those who give their lives for God's glory by reaching out to the broken and needy, the ranks of those whose overriding desire in life is to be His instruments.

An Introduction: "So You Want to Go Back to Egypt?"

One of my Dad's favorite Keith Green songs, "So You Want to Go Back to Egypt," suggests the resistance that meets Jesus' bluntness about the radical Christian calling. You can't say Jesus didn't warn us:

"Foxes have dens and birds have nests, but the Son of Man has no place to lay his head" (Luke 9:62).

"Let the dead bury their own dead, but you, go and proclaim the kingdom of God" (Luke 9:58).

"No one who puts a hand to the plow and looks back is fit for service in the kingdom of God" (Luke 9:62).

A person pondering missions might conjure in his imagination insects, strange food, and cultural imponderables. These are all true. But our great God has promised to any who are willing, "I will never leave you or forsake you" (Joshua 1:5; Deuteronomy 31:6-8).

With no formal training I showed up with a few other green-behind-the-ears types in "The Pearl of Africa," as Winston Churchill dubbed the East African country in better days. I had recently given my life to the Lord after reading Dietrich Bonhoeffer's *The Cost of Discipleship,* when it just so happened that a handful of refugees fleeing Idi Amin landed in the pews of my home church, New Life Presbyterian in Glenside, Pennsylvania. They urged my pastor to send a team to help rebuild their country, and as a newly minted believer I was among those who accepted the call.

With no instructions except to listen to the leadership of the church in Uganda and to "fit in the best we could," we read the promise of Jesus in Matthew 19:29, that "whoever leaves homes, and parents, and families for my name's sake will receive a hundredfold more in this life and inherit eternal life." We decided to simply believe it.

The pages you are about to read will give you insight into our challenges over the subsequent three years, challenges beyond what a man is prepared to cope with in human strength alone. As the Apostle Paul once said, "Indeed, we felt that we had received the sentence of death. But that was to make us rely, not on ourselves, but on God who raises the dead" (2 Corinthians 1:9).

God ran interference repeatedly, not only protecting and providing, but bringing about much fruit from those early steps of faith and obedience. We found experientially that no matter the circumstances, God was able (Ephesians 3:20). The first church that was planted by my then pastor Jack Miller has in turn multiplied assemblies throughout the nation.

Early in my stay in Uganda, the U.S. Embassy sought me out and told me they could not protect me, and that I should flee the country. Right or wrong, I stayed. They were not able to protect, but God was.

Our heavenly Father covered me with his Spirit and never left me. I sensed His presence even in the strangest dilemmas. As a man named David said long ago:

"In the LORD I take refuge. How can you then say to me, 'Flee like a bird to your mountain'…?" (Psalm 11:1).

I want to encourage you to listen to the Holy Spirit if He speaks to you today (Hebrews 3:15). If you do this, you will live as you are meant to live. If He is leading you out of Egypt, I encourage you to go. "The harvest is plentiful, but the laborers are few; therefore pray earnestly to the Lord of the harvest to send out more laborers" (Matthew 9:37). You may just find yourself a laborer on the adventure of your life.

So You Wanna Go Back to Egypt

Keith Green

So you want to go back to Egypt/ Where it's warm and secure

Are you sorry you bought the one way ticket/ When you thought you were sure

You wanted to live in the land of promise/ But now it's getting so hard

Are you sorry you're out here in the desert/ Instead of your own backyard

Eating leeks and onions by the Nile/ Ooh, what breath for dining out in style

Ooh, my life is on the skids/ Building the pyramids

Well, there's nothing to do but travel/ And we sure travel a lot

'Cause it's hard to keep your feet from moving/ When the sand gets so hot

And in the morning, it's manna hotcakes/ We snack on manna all day

And we sure had a winner last night for dinner/ Flaming manna souffle

Well, we once complained about something new to munch/ The ground opened up and had some of us for lunch

Oo, such fire and smoke, Can't God even take a joke? Huh?

No!

So you want to go back to Egypt/ Where your friends wait for you

You can throw a big party and tell the whole gang/ Of what they said was all true

And this Moses acts like a bigshot/ Who does he think he is?

Well it's true that God works lots of miracles/ But Moses thinks they're his

Oh we're having so much trouble even now/ Why'd he get so mad about the cow

Moses seems rather idle/ He just sits around and writes the Bible!

Oh Moses put down your pen? What?

Oh no manna again? Oh, manna waffles

Manna burgers

Manna bagels

Filet of manna

Manna patty

BaManna bread!

1. Eno Uganda

"Duka! Duka!" they yelled in the Luganda tribal language. Awoken from sleep at the break of dawn, Alan and I were hurried out of the house. We found ourselves standing in a crowd haphazardly corralled by soldiers in camouflage. A Tanzanian fighter had been killed, and the whole army marched to Kampala to mete out consequences. I had no time to retrieve my passport for protection.

In the still silhouetted morning there was a machine gun pointing at me and a soldier ordering me to run. Two men pleading for their lives were silenced with the sickening sound of gunshots. We realized we were not in control. Had my God left me?

In past harassments, my Ugandan friends and I had often whispered to each other, "Eno Uganda," or "This is Uganda." Uganda is a place where the surreal happens and nothing is predictable. How many times had we begged, "Lord, don't leave me now."

It was 1980 and the brutal government of Idi Amin had been overthrown in a coup with the help of the Tanzanian army. The army had stayed to help, trying to keep the peace while a new regime prepared to take the reins. But the three post-Amin years were far from peaceful. Dead bodies lay in the streets. Roadblocks disrupted travel and instilled fear, checkpoint soldiers looking for bribes. Night and day, gunfire was heard. There was a curfew, but it offered scant protection.

If your thoughts did settle down, you were reminded of your empty stomach. We had no salt, no sugar, no cheese, nothing "fun" to eat. We resorted to relief packages from the U.S. marked "Not for Human Consumption." Sustenance intended to fatten pigs was sent off to Uganda as humanitarian aid!

Earlier, on this night when the soldiers taught us who was in charge, I had been lying on the floor with my fellow missionary Alan next to me, a candle to light the darkness. We had heard bombs going off and AK-47 rifle rounds in the distance. We supped on food meant for animal troughs, made marginally palatable by dipping it into a watery red curry "soup." Our souls were filled with Psalms and other Scriptures.

Finally, I slipped into bed with my hand on my heart. I had to prove it was still beating. "Lord," I prayed slowly, "if you leave me now…." I stopped there for this was unthinkable, and fell asleep. When I awoke to the sound of gunfire my hand was still on my chest. The rude warning knock on the door did not succeed in overcoming my assurance that God would never leave me.

Forty-five years later, I sit in the U.S. contemplating how I lived through a war zone in this landlocked East African nation ringed by Kenya, Sudan, the Democratic Republic of the Congo, Rwanda, and Tanzania. There had been seven Americans registered in the entire country. The U.S. Embassy had found me and warned me to leave, not able to promise protection. Something inside told me I should not leave, I should stay. So I did.

The government would be overthrown two more times in those early years after Amin, and would be overthrown a fourth time after my return to the States to resume my studies. During our turbulent sojourn my friends and I would ask ourselves, "Will the replacement government be more benign? Less corrupt? Will 'The Pearl of Africa,' as Winston Churchill called Uganda, return to the relative peace and prosperity it once enjoyed?

Hebrews 13:5-6 Keep your lives free from the love of money and be content with what you have, because God has said, "Never will I leave you; never will I forsake you."

2. Jjaja Muwanga

Who do you turn to in times of need? The answer seems obvious: God.

But under pressure --- of human depravity, of lack of food, or shelter --- one's sureties are challenged, and the depths of faith's foundations tested.

Uganda was and is a place of poverty. Poverty engenders hopelessness. Hopelessness, in turn, a search for answers. Witchcraft is where many Ugandans turn in hopelessness. They align themselves with evil spirits, and spirits are capable of real impact.

Transportation in our early days of ministry was unreliable to nonexistent, so we often walked miles to our destinations. At the end of one long day I was headed to my home in Busega, east of Kampala, and came upon a shop that sells wood. Many of the roads in Kampala are lined with such small shops, typically constructed of something like driftwood and tin scraps.

Wanting to rest a few minutes, I struck up a conversation with the owner. He kept his wood out front, hopeful that passersby would make a purchase. I wondered to myself if he took the time and effort to move those boards in and out every day. I mean, "Eno Uganda!" Even in broad daylight things are stolen.

Samuel, the shop owner, proudly told me he could leave the wood outdoors all night and never lose a board. This was because he prayed to a "Jjaja Muwanga," a witch doctor known throughout Uganda. Jjaja Muwanga practiced voodoo-like sorcery using charms and other paraphernalia. Samuel explained that if anyone dared take a board, he would be caught by Jaja Mwanga in a spell and paralyzed all night long. When the owner arrived in the morning, he would escort the thief to the police and have him punished to the maximum extent of the law.

I told Samuel I was impressed by his story, but that my God was more powerful than his witch doctor. My God can forgive a person of his sins and give him eternal life. Samuel was instantly angry with me, this 20-year-old white guy with hubris, and said: "I will send Jjaja Muwanga to your house tonight to beat you and beat you and beat you." I calmly pointed to the village and told him exactly where I lived. I also told him my orphans and I would be praying for him to come to know Jesus as his Lord and Savior.

When I arrived at my house I brought my orphans together and said, "I may have gotten us into a little trouble." I proceeded to relate the incident at the local market. We then had a worship service and praised God loudly, asking Him to station his angels around our home to protect us. I proceeded to have the best night's sleep ever, and rejoiced in the morning that no evil had befallen us.

Two weeks later my young men and I headed to church. While waiting for transportation into town, I spotted the shop owner at a distance. He was dressed in a suit, and I called to him. "Hey Samuel!" He looked over to me. I continued, "I didn't realize you worship Jjaja Muwanga in the church!" He came running and enthusiastically shared his story: "Ever since that day, all the powers of Jjaja Muwanga left me, and now I am a follower of Jesus Christ!" We all rejoiced with him and continued on to church, where I stood up and shared these events with the congregation, who clapped loudly.

Why all the joy? All in attendance were reflecting on where they had come from. I had seen many services where former slaves of darkness surrendered their spiritual charms and witchcraft paraphernalia, burning and demolishing them as they gave their lives to Christ. Hopelessness was turned to joy.

Romans 15:13 NIV "May the God of hope fill you with all joy and peace in believing, so that by the power of the Holy Spirit you may abound in hope."

3. The Austrian

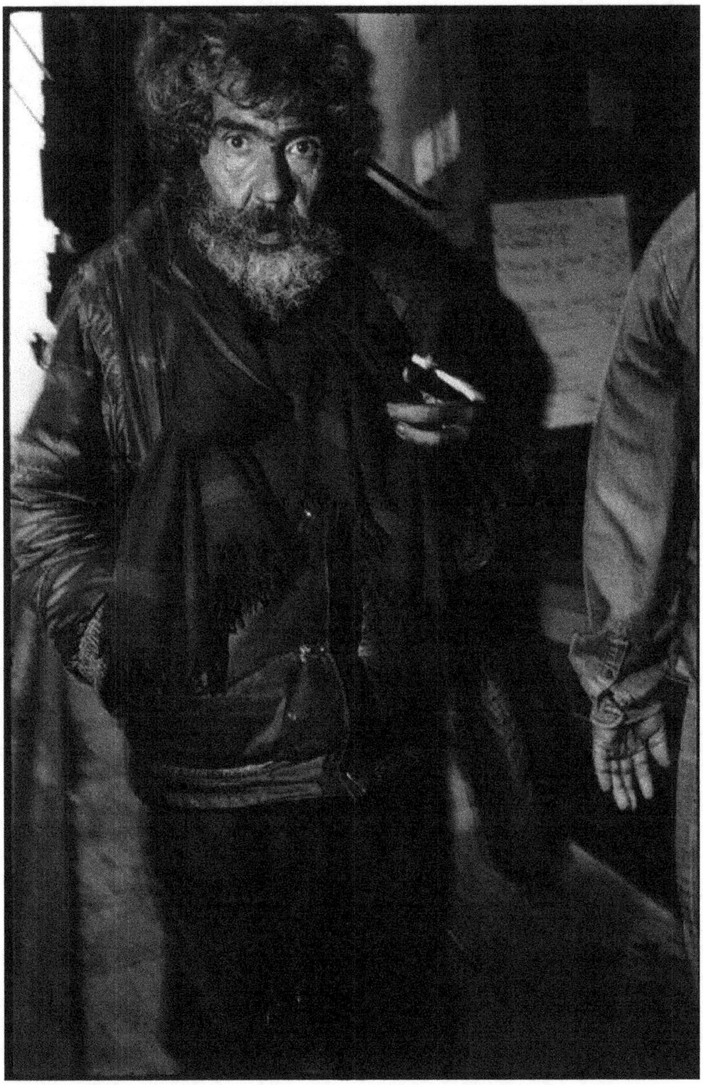

Weakness is a felt presence in Uganda. One goes without food, a place to lay one's head, clean water for bathing.

Franz, from Austria, was an unkempt man who wandered into Uganda after leaving his wife and family. He fit in with the poorest of the poor. How does a man get to this point, especially a "muzungu" ("foreigner")?

One day as my painters and I were walking to the industrial park to paint offices of the local petroleum company, I spotted him sipping tea at "Chia," an open-air restaurant. I sat down with him and said that I was on my way to work but would stop by on my return trip. When I did, in the course of our conversation Franz showed me where he was sleeping --- out in the open with no protection from nighttime street gangs. I offered him a gun that my workers had found while we were landscaping. He gladly accepted it.

Time went by and I didn't see Franz again on my route to work. I sometimes wondered what had become of him. Had he fallen prey to the broods of the night? Had he starved to death? Had he gone back to his wife and children to make amends?

Three months later an open-top Humvee came trundling into our church parking area. Out stepped Franz, properly dressed and in a state of orderliness, almost unrecognizable. He pulled me out of the service and to the church grounds, and with enthusiasm handed me seven $100 bills. Even today in Uganda this would be considered a large sum.

How could this man, only three months ago an indigent, come by this kind of money? Franz explained that Isaiah tells us God's people will "beat their swords into plowshares," and that that is what he had done. He had traded the gun for a toolbox and opened a mechanic shop in the industrial center. His business had grown so much that he had more than he could use, and wanted to bless me for giving him the gun.

Franz then got back into his Humvee and drove off in a cloud of red dirt. Ten orphans under my care who had no means of support were the beneficiaries of the largess of Uganda's least likely inhabitant.

Six weeks later Franz reappeared. Though successful in business, he had trouble finding trustworthy employees. I delightedly explained to Franz that one of my purposes in Uganda was to help church members obtain careers. In those days in Uganda, unemployment was at 80% and a job was like gold.

I quickly started a training course for our church members and taught them biblical principles for becoming excellent employees. Attributes like honesty, integrity, and trustworthiness were implanted in their thinking. I began sending workers to Franz, who in turn continued to bless our home with supplies. The church we planted was buzzing with excitement over God's doings.

In ministry, and in our daily life, when we take time to make people feel recognized, showing no partiality, we find that God can use anyone. His power is displayed in human weakness.

2 Corinthians 12: 9-10 NIV "My grace is sufficient for you, for my power is made perfect in weakness. Therefore I will boast all the more gladly about my weaknesses, so that Christ's power may rest on me. That is why, for Christ's sake, I delight in weaknesses, in insults, in hardships, in persecutions, in difficulties. For when I am weak, then I am strong."

4. The Busega Home

Little children on the street; begging, pleading, and needing food. Some became mean due to the lack of discipline and the fear of not knowing where or when a meal might come to them, or where they might lay their head in safety to sleep. Others became soft and laid themselves there to pass into the next life, disfigured by hunger and malnourishment. Even if they had a mirror they might not recognize themselves. Orphans caused by the great reign of terror through the infamous Idi Amin. His ruling was so vicious that he was known as the "Butcher of Uganda." Throughout his time in power tens of thousands of men and women were forcibly taken from their homes and thrown in the back of a pickup truck, never to be seen again. Families broken, and children who were held by their father and mother that morning, became orphans of the street that same day's night.

Many of these prisoners were taken to Amin's torture chamber in Nakasero, Kampala, where they faced the cruelty of one man's desire to reign without threat. I once visited this site, and my eyes will never forget the buckets of blood, and feces, and urine spread on the walls and floors. The stench was still too awful to describe to this day. Oh, I can't imagine what these people suffered.

To wear glasses was a death wish. Amin was very paranoid of anyone who wore glasses because they likely could read. Anyone who was learned enough to read was also intelligent enough to plan the ruler’s death. That man must go! Amin felt threatened all the time and would kill without hesitation to maintain his power.

As a result, the marketplace and streets and bus parks were overrun by 'bayaye' children or 'children of the street.' They would sleep under buses at night to get warmth from the engines. During the day, these children, without parents, would sell cigarettes one by one, or they would pickpocket people shopping in the open-air markets. Some were malicious and even evil. Others were just trying to survive. Either way, they all were homeless and desperate.

The leadership of the First Presbyterian Church of Uganda asked me to look after some of these children whom the church had befriended. It was my job to prayerfully find a house and take some of these youth in. At age 21, I now had 10 children to look after, feed and clothe, and get into schools. The Lord provided me with a home owned by Bishop Gonahasa, who became a great friend. Although the home was in the slums of Kampala, the 5 bedroom house, with minimal amenities, provided us with some basic shelter for only $15 per month. Even so, this could be a struggle, with the lack of jobs in the city. We lived on that acre of land peaceably for almost 2 full years.

One child was dropped at my doorstep with a note from the mother, that she could not care for him and gave me the responsibility for his life. These children became life-long friends. This particular child was eventually able to find his way to the United States as an adult, and has a wife and three children whom he supports as a truck driver. I am still working with others in Uganda. Unfortunately, some have died from the AIDs epidemic and even one was killed only years after I left Uganda, but some have prospered in this world and own businesses and have raised families. Even now, some of their children work alongside our missions' teams and support us as translators and guides. How God worked through just a willing spirit still amazes me, as I know these things were not of my own doing.

Part of these blessings were that one of the church leaders was also the government agent assigned the duty of Minister of Rehabilitation and Youth. This status allowed him to provide me with a soldier to help protect our home since I was helping look after these lost and homeless children. Although the soldier was often drunk with 'waragi' (also known as 'kasese'), the local alcohol, the protection provided us with a safe place to lay our heads. The first night we were there, the soldier found it necessary to protect us and had to kill someone who was looking to enter the grounds. I warned him though to please only do this if it was absolutely necessary for our lives.

The children and I each had daily chores to run and gather water for the household and to keep the property nice and clean. We tilled the grounds and grew lots of food to help feed the eleven of us. Corn and avocado were plentiful once we took the time to weed the property and plant seeds. We also raised chickens. After school we enjoyed many joyful times playing sports on the property.

These boys, lovingly known to me as *Busega Boys*, relied on me, and I on them throughout these years. I tried to teach them right from wrong. I spent many nights praying with them and reading Scripture. I grew up very quickly in those two years, but I felt I was following the words of James, the brother of Jesus, when he said, to look after the orphans and widows in their distress (James 1:27).

Adjacent to our property was the gravesite of 'Mackay of Uganda,' the very first missionary to 'The Pearl of Africa'. I often visited that site for inspiration. These missionaries came over from England by boat. Half died along the way, and the rest died doing the mission of sharing the good news of Jesus Christ to this great country in Africa. What an honor to now be a missionary right at the same place that the first missionary once shared the gospel! Now it was 'my turn' and I welcomed the opportunity.

James 1:27 NIV "Religion that God our Father accepts as pure and faultless is this: to look after orphans and widows in their distress and to keep oneself from being polluted by the world."

5. You've Got to be Kidding Me!

Being understood in the present should not be the driving force of a missionary. Relationships through friendship and care should be the goal. God will supply the timing and the resources for everything else.

As a Westerner I came to Uganda thinking I could change whatever ailed the country, by my faith and my dedication to making a difference in the lives of those I met. I believed I just needed to "roll up my sleeves," "sharpen my pencil," and "get the job done," as my Mom had taught me.

But every step of the way there were obstacles. I found myself getting easily irritated by how things were done, insulted by the way people treated me --- and, in the end, angry to realize that it was I, not they, who needed to change.

I can't help but compare my frustration to that of Jesus when the disciples continually failed to grasp his Person and mission (John 8:43; 13:19; 14:29; 16:1-4; 20:9; Luke 2:50; 18:34; Mark 4:13; 8:21; 9:32). He knew they would understand in the future (John 13:7; Luke 24:45), but for the present their expectations were worldly with regard to how God supplies needs. Nor did they fathom that Jesus had come to serve them.

Once I brought a mechanic to my Land Rover that had broken down, only to find the deacons of the church siphoning gas out of my truck! I asked them why they were doing that, and their reply was that since I wasn't using the gas, they would. How could they do this? Why in the world did they think I had come to this country in the first place? The very people who were supposed to be on my side were draining me of the little resources I had.

Another time I took my truck in for repairs. I was told that I had to provide the oil for the shop myself. The mechanics took the bolt off to drain the old oil out, and forgot to put the plug back in. They poured the oil that I had provided into the engine, and it all drained into the dirt. Then they asked *me* to provide more oil, though it was their mistake! They also removed some perfectly usable car parts from under the hood and replaced them with junk parts.

Many times people would just happen to drop by at mealtime. I was slow to catch on, but the fact is that people had to find meals to survive, so it was a common practice to show up at a person's house if you thought the occupants had food to spare. Sometimes these impromptu visitors would be fine with waiting two hours in hopes of a bite. I started to resent their visits and shook my head in disgust when I saw them coming.

A local church leader stopped by my house and went into my cornfields and loaded up three big armfuls of my corn without even coming in to say hello! I watched incredulously from inside my house. He then proceeded to sit me down and rebuke me for not taking enough time with the widows who did their sewing in front of the church, and for merely waving to them and saying "Good morning."

In the USA my greeting to the ladies would have been considered gracious. In Uganda, where life is slower paced, I apparently was insulting them by not greeting each woman individually. My indignant response was "Are you kidding me! No wonder they have poverty! Everyone is just sitting around and not making good use of the time!"

These brutal encounters with culture did not return empty. I had considered myself sent by God to serve. But if I had looked more closely, I would have seen that I was frustrated because I was serving myself. As a missionary I finally came to learn that one has to meet people where they are. Matthew 15:32 states that Jesus looked upon the crowd with compassion, because they were like sheep without a shepherd. I needed to regard what I had considered disturbances and ill-mannered behavior as opportunities for love.

After all, how could someone hear my words about a God who satisfies all, while their stomachs ached with hunger? How could they understand grace while I judged their mistakes? How could they believe that God provides daily when I was more concerned about the gas in my car for tomorrow and not God's faithfulness in the troubles of today?

One Ugandan finally sat me down in love and told me, “Uganda didn’t get this way overnight. It will take time for the country to be great again.” I then realized that my awful attitude was what needed to change. Otherwise, nothing good would come from my time there.

Matthew 15:32 NIV “Jesus called his disciples to him and said, ‘I have compassion for these people; they have already been with me three days and have nothing to eat. I do not want to send them away hungry, or they may collapse on the way.’”

6. My Amazing Father

Words can only begin to express what an amazing father I had. I learned everything I know about the body of Christ and its diversity from him. So many Saturdays, as a youth, I would wake up to find people from another country joining us for breakfast. They would tell us of how God was working in their country. I was always struck by how their lives seemed different from my own, having none of the material blessings and security I had come to take as normal.

Often, I would sit there and listen to their stories, and hear how their faith had been tested. They had faced challenges in just meeting the basic needs of their families, yet exuded a quiet confidence, to a level I had not experienced. What did they know, I wondered. They also frequently offered an invitation to visit them.

My dear father traveled extensively to Africa, South America, Haiti, and other developing countries. He brought home pictures of the places he visited, and at night would tell us "Chinese missionary stories." I lay in bed listening, and picturing what life overseas would be like.

This man who raised me showed me how to act like God intended. Jesus met people where they had need. Like Jesus, my father went to countries where the living conditions were poor. He dined with undesirables. He sat with a family of seven or eight who shared one egg cut into little pieces. He ate what was placed in front of him, no matter if the local delicacy was unrecognizable to the American eye.

There is a song I like to sing called "The Woman at the Well," based on John 4:7-26. How remarkable that a Jewish man, and one of considerable social standing, would not only talk to this outcast Samaritan woman but relate to her. I often imagined the joy people must have felt when my father showed up. My father used to say that "showing up" was 90% of missions.

Once you "show up," the next important aspect of missions is relying on God. What did Jesus do in private? He prayed. As I observed my father's daily routine, I noticed him rise in the middle of the night, get on his knees by his bed, and talk to God. He prayed for his family and for the needy all over the world. On Saturday nights Dad and Mom would set aside thirty minutes in prayer for pastors near and far who were preparing for the Lord's Day. Anyone who happened to be in the house at the time was welcome to join them.

Once, early in my life, Dad had a one-on-one conversation with me that I will never forget. "Steve, there are some things in your life that I don't condone. But I want you to know that I love you unconditionally." From that moment forward, I knew I was loved, special, and acceptable. I realized I was able to do the many things my Dad trained and taught me about ministering the hope of the gospel in foreign countries. His unconditional love set me in motion. And he loved me like that to the day of his passing.

I was motivated to live a God-fearing life because of how my father lived and persevered. He followed the command of Colossians 3:17, to do and say all things in the name of Jesus, giving God the glory. He stepped out in faith, often and confidently, not knowing the end results. By this example he equipped me to have faith and to give everything I had for the sake of the gospel.

My Dad's example gave me courage to start businesses and to teach others the godly ways to run a business. His "going into all the world to preach the gospel" inspired me to step out and share the hope of a Savior who cares for all of us, even the weak.

In 1982 my Dad came to war-torn Uganda to visit me. He knew life there was dangerous, but his love for one of his five children made him take the risk. With his harmonica always at the ready, he led the congregation in song in the local church that we planted. He stayed at my Busega Home and taught the orphans to play the recorder that he had brought with him.

When my Dad boarded the plane in the bullet-ridden Entebbe airport to return to the USA, tears came to my eyes because the person so critical to the person I had become was leaving me. For a moment my heart felt empty. Later, he told me he had shed tears too. Many times throughout that first three-year stint in Uganda I asked myself whenever I was in a tough spot, "What would my Dad do in this situation?"

In 2023 my father went to be with the Lord. I have his picture next to my bed for inspiration. I told him on his last day on earth, as he was holding my shirt, "Dad, anything good that has come from my life has been because of your unconditional love. Thank you so very much, my dear amazing father, for that unspeakable blessing."

Hopefully, you have parents who are godly examples. But if you do not, I encourage you to find a man older than you or a godly christian woman in your life. On the mission field, we will fail many times, but going back to the basics of showing up and relying on God can replenish the storehouses of servanthood.

Psalm 119:105 "Your Word is a lamp for my feet, and a light unto my path."

Me and my Dad

7. Presbyterian Church in Uganda Painting Company

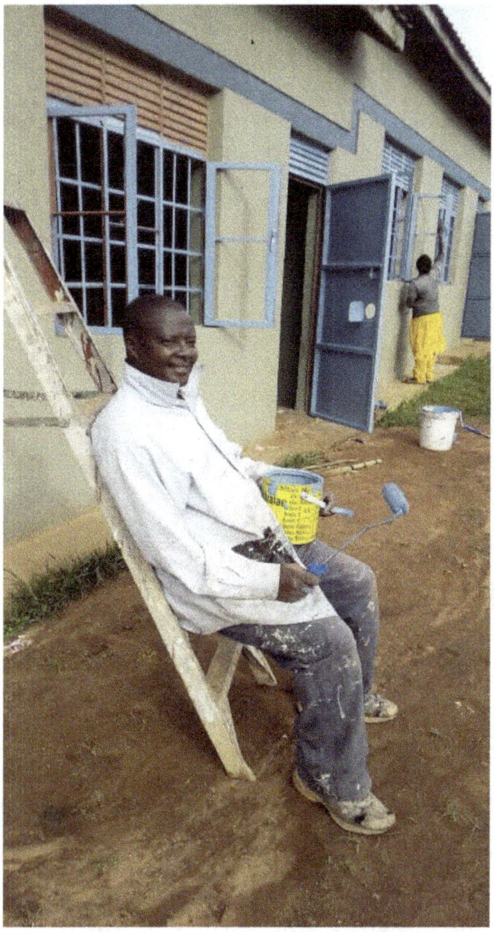

Under the guidance of both my Ugandan and American church leadership, it was decided that we should bring the good news of the gospel in both "word and deed." We would go out into the streets preaching to anyone who would listen throughout Kampala, the capital of Uganda. Then we would try to meet that person's needs, not only spiritual but material needs. One of the ways we thought to do this was by starting a business that would employ people.

When we first came to Uganda, the country's unemployment was 80%. If you had one of the few jobs available, you were paid roughly the equivalent of fifty American cents per day. So for a day's labor, you could buy a loaf of bread, hardly adequate to feed a family of five, six, seven, or more.

Before coming to Uganda I had started a small painting company in the States, and the church leadership suggested it would be a good idea to start one in Uganda. Before we launched the company in Uganda, we had to decide whether it would be church-operated or run independently. We settled on running the business through the church, with the goal of letting it run independently once church members were experienced enough to take over.

There was much need for a painting business in Kampala, but the challenges were numerous. Public transportation was underdeveloped, so it was impossible to rely on it to get to and from the project sites. We would need reliable and ample gas, but the country's supply was scarce.

To put fuel in a vehicle, one was required to get approval from two government officials. Then you would need to find the funds to pay for it.

Even if transportation were reliable, there was no paint in any stores. The only way to get paint was to have it donated to us --- or to make it ourselves! Lastly, finding a company or person with the funds to support our venture was almost impossible. The mismanagement of the country by its former dictator, Idi Amin, had left it in shambles.

How do we get paint when there is none? The Lord had a plan. A sister church back in the states supplied us with three fifty-gallon drums. That donation helped us launch the first church-run painting enterprise in the country. We praised God.

However, we had only three colors to paint with, and one was green, which had limited appeal to the local community. We decided to use up the unwanted green in training our new painters, who would enhance the houses of the congregation. So an American volunteer named John Songster and I made the paint serve double duty as practice and simultaneously a blessing on our church members.

Our painters learned the three "L's" of painting: Lots of paint on your brush; Long strokes to make it smooth and rich-looking; Light touch so there is an equal amount of mileage on the surfaces being painted. We were now ready to step out and paint the town.

To get contracts, John and I went to the big petroleum companies in the industrial center. We personally introduced our company and asked for projects. One good thing about these companies was that they were large enough to have the necessary paint to complete the needed improvements on their buildings. They just needed the laborers.

We still had a learning curve, with our semi-skilled paint crew. We were given a two-part varnish and hardening kit from Esso (Exxon here in the USA), and our guys neglected to mix in the hardener! Esso executives kept asking me when the varnish was going to dry, and I assured them it would very soon. But two days later it was still tacky, and I checked with my foreman and discovered they had not combined the Part A and Part B (hardener). We had to strip the sealant off and start all over. It was a huge setback to our reputation as the "Presbyterian Church of Uganda Painting Company."

On another occasion we had been given a special silver paint by Caltex (Texaco) to apply to the exterior of big oil tanks. We took on the job even though we had no ladders, no sprayers, and no experience in rolling on this metallic style of paint. We found a way, but unfortunately, the process of rolling on paint in many directions (It should have been applied by sprayer) left unsightly roller marks. Another setback.

Undaunted, we persevered and started landing more and more jobs. Because we didn't quit, companies saw value in hiring us, even with our flaws. As our company grew, we needed to make our own paint in order to accomplish the many projects coming our way. The closest place to get paint chemicals was in Kenya's capital, Nairobi.

My longtime friend, Bob Heppe, and I borrowed a vehicle for the 300-mile trek to Nairobi (plus 300 miles back). But we would have to find gas for such a long trip. Providentially, the church had connections with some higher-ranking government officials and were able to obtain the required signatures to purchase fuel.

It took us three days of standing in line to get to the gas pump. When we finally reached the front of the line, we were told to our dismay that there was "no more gas." A whole day had been wasted in waiting, and the petrol had been sold elsewhere (the black market). At long last we managed somehow to acquire it and started off on the long return trip to Kampala, with the know-how and ingredients to concoct our own paint.

How much I had taken for granted living in the United States! In America I can place an order for a hundred gallons and have it delivered to the job site the same morning. I can fill my truck, anywhere and anytime, then drive it over smooth, well-constructed and maintained roads.

The challenges we faced every step of the way underscored God's incredible provision in allowing us to keep the paint company afloat. Twenty men have been able to feed their families for the past 40 years, even to this day, due to the perseverance of our team. Two of the young men who worked on those projects have joined me in West Africa to minister by painting one of the only Christian schools in that Muslim country.

Besides providing for a score of families, the company started to make good profits. In this way we were able to hand over large sums to the deacons of the church, who in turn distributed aid to many widows whose husbands had been killed under Amin. Orphans were also helped with proceeds of the PCU Paint company.

2 Thessalonians 3:10 NIV "For even when we were with you, we gave you this rule: 'The one who is unwilling to work shall not eat.'"

Ephesians 4:28 NIV "Anyone who has been stealing must steal no longer, but must work, doing something useful with their own hands, that they may have something to share with those in need."

8. Jack Miller

Dr. Jack Miller was passionate about the Kingdom of God and the importance of living radically for Christ. Whenever he preached in the early days, I would ask myself, "What will I do with today's message?" Every sermon was focused on what a Savior we have in Jesus Christ and what power he has to forgive our sins. He reasoned that because of Christ's accomplishment on Calvary, we can go anywhere to live out our faith, and He will be with us every step of the way.

Jack and his wife Rose Marie first started a Bible study in their home in the 1970s, and over the years their home church grew --- not because they sought after the affluent or the political influencers, but because they sought out those in need. To be sure, all of us are in need of the saving grace of the Lord, and no doubt are all poor. It can't be denied, however, that there is a particular hopelessness that comes with physical, psychological, and monetary need. It was people with these types of problems that Jack reached out to; he invited those whom the world rejected.

Jack was humble, one could almost say, self-deprecating. But he was enamored of a Savior who can move mountains. He is one of four men whom I deeply respect who have gone home to be with the Lord. After Jack died, a close friend of his called me, full of sadness. This man was a well-known professor at a Christian college, and himself a trailblazer who took teams of students to Uganda over a period of thirty years. He said of Jack, “I would give my own life up to have Jack back on earth. The Church has many teachers, but so few evangelists.”

Jack did not teach theory but living out the gospel. He was convicted by the call to “go into all the world and preach the gospel” (Mark 16:15). Acts 1:8 tells us that the mandate is not just local but to “the ends of the earth.” What Jack began in the neighborhood, he extended to the bustling street corners of Philadelphia like Broad and Olney, then expanded it across continents to Ireland, London, and, yes, Africa.

Jack was interested in the whole man. Jesus had died for our soul’s salvation but also cared about us having enough to eat (He fed the 5,000), and being physically well (He healed all those who asked of Him). He cared about the storms in our lives, as proved by the way he calmed the winds and waves on the Sea of Galilee. Jack never shrank from challenging the congregation to not only understand the gospel with their minds but to go in the strength of the Lord and live it out. Not only preach but to minister to bodies and souls.

Starting in the mid-seventies, Idi Amin and his henchmen persecuted the Ugandan church, forcing many to flee for their lives. In the late seventies a small group of pastors managed to escape by the hand of God. God had a plan for these refugees, and a few who landed in the suburbs of Philadelphia found themselves taking classes at Westminster Theological Seminary, where Jack was a professor.

Among them was a Ugandan pastor and politician named Reverend Kefa Sempangi, who asked Jack to send some of the church back with him to Uganda to help with rebuilding once the dictatorship ended. Jack was ready to act.

While some criticized Jack and thought him foolhardy, he was not moved by people's opinions but by the voice of the Spirit, and stepped out in faith despite danger and lack of resources. When Amin was finally deposed and banished from Uganda, Jack seized the moment and asked those of us on his Philadelphia preaching team to prayerfully consider leaving our comfort zones and joining him in Uganda. We embarked in 1979, less than a year after Amin's ouster. Our instructions were simple: immerse ourselves in the people, get our cues from the local church, and fit in by helping to meet physical and spiritual needs of the people.

During our time there, Jack and the Ugandan church leadership planted the First Presbyterian Church of Uganda in Kampala. It would become the mother church of other assemblies planted in the following years. Jack instilled a spirit of evangelism and spurred on the beginnings of what became known as the "Back to God Crusades." These campaigns continued after Jack left the country, with the local church traveling near and far to preach the gospel.

Sometimes we would combine evangelism and service by doing "garbage truck evangelism." A few of us would preach and give testimony about the Lord, and the rest of us would be shoveling the big mounds of waste piled up throughout Kampala. Many came to know the Lord as a result of those early days of preaching and doing service.

As of 2023 there are 88 churches that have been planted throughout Uganda, all birthed from this original 1979 plant. The General Assembly recently met in Northern Uganda (Gulu), where pastors from all four corners of Uganda reflected on God's goodness and planned for the years to come. All because of how God used the faith and vision of a man I will forever respect, Jack Miller.

Jack was a trailblazer. He was a pioneer in "outgrowing the ingrown church," which became the title of his 1986 book. He was a man of prayer, whether we were discussing some upcoming outreach in Uganda, or sprawled on the floor when gunfire rained over our house. Jack would say, "Let's just pray about this."

Some would criticize Jack for not spending enough time at the church he was hired to pastor. But he wisely knew that part of being a true pastor was modeling the gospel for his congregation. He made disciples like me, challenging us to be salt and light in a hurting world.

Over the three years I lived in Uganda, since all of us were learning on the job, there was occasional tension between Jack and myself, which were mostly due to my youth and immaturity. But through it all, I admired Jack's determination to further the kingdom of

God. When I was finally headed to the airport at the end of those first years, Jack rode with me. Along the way, he and I were sitting in the back seat, and Jack touched my arm and said, "Steve, you should have a good feeling about these last three years. God was with you, and He did many good things because of you being here."

Thank you, Lord, for your servant Jack.

Matthew 28:19 NIV "Therefore, go and make disciples of all nations, baptizing them in the name of the Father and of the Son."

9. The Cost of Ministry

Stepping onto an airplane for a six-week trip to help plant the first church in the Presbyterian movement of Uganda: How did I get here? Did I even realize the comforts of home I would miss? Did I know the dangers I would face?

I was mindful of the writings of a Lutheran pastor in 1940s Germany who exhorted the Church, "Seek ye first the Kingdom of God and His righteousness." Dietrich Bonhoeffer lived in safety before he spoke out against Adolf Hitler's extermination of the Jewish people. He could easily have kept silent and hoped that the relative peace he and his fiancée enjoyed would last. But he decided there was no way to stand by and watch. The decision cost him his life at the age of 39: death by hanging on April 9,1945, three weeks before Hitler's own death on April 30th ended the Nazi reign of terror and the Western front of WWII.

Bonhoeffer's 1937 book *The Cost of Discipleship* greatly influenced my life. He challenged the Church to leave the comforts of this world, which no one can really hold on to, and to trade it for an eternity that no one can take away. I read these words at a tender point in my life, and told my Dad, "If Christianity is real, something major is missing in my life. And with all humility, I would say that something is missing in the lives of many Christians I know."

My Dad was pleased, discerning that the Holy Spirit was working in my heart. For these are the struggles that reside in the heart of any true missionary: At what cost is the life of ministry? At what cost the servanthood of the Most High? Bonhoeffer noted: "Everyone who has left houses or brothers or sisters or father or mother or wife or children or fields for my sake will receive a hundred times as much and will inherit eternal life" (Matthew 19:29).

When Jack Miller asked me to join his team, those words of Christ in Matthew were working in my heart. I agreed to board a plane to East Africa equipped with nothing but the promises of God. I left my studies and had very little money, but I believed I was going in the power of the Holy Spirit and the reality that God is able to do beyond anything I could ask or imagine (Ephesians 3:20). His resources would be enough.

God's Word proved trustworthy. What was supposed to be a six-week stint in Uganda turned into a three-year, feet-on-the-ground ministry. And it has continued to be a part of what the Lord is doing in Uganda and in my heart over 40 years.

Luke 14:25-33 NIV "Jesus said, 'Anyone who does not renounce all that he has cannot be my disciple.'"

10. You Don't Love Me!

To continue with "the cost of ministry," health is one of the precious things at risk when you serve in a developing country. Conditions in Uganda were harsh for a person coming from a cushy home like mine in the U.S. Food was scarce, there was no refrigeration, no one spoke English, and you went on foot everywhere you wanted to go. Water was hard to get, to say nothing of running water. You would have to trek a far distance to get "Jerry cans" filled at the well.

Water! What an essential resource! To this day, lack of clean water, especially in the villages, makes it nearly impossible to keep clean and healthy. I never really got clean. There was no shower to stand under; there was no knob to make the temperature hotter or colder. At most I would get a rare splashing over the red dirt on my body. Even this wasn't a relief, as the moistening of clay reacts with the skin to cause uncontrollable itching. It would take a half hour after my bird bath for the intense itching and inflammation to stop.

When you are surrounded by people whose language you do not understand, and you are hungry, itchy, and tired, the last thing you want is sickness on top of that. I think I held it together for the most part until my fifth bout with malaria (which wouldn't be my last) became my breaking point.

The first time I had malaria I was throwing up violently and landed in a local hospital. There they injected me with a thick syrupy medicine through a reused needle; it felt like a blunt pencil being shoved into me. As we drove away from the hospital I threw up out of the truck one last time for good measure, and the sickness passed.

This fifth time I was in the village with my orphans and was hit with a more extreme case than in the past. I alternated vomiting and diarrhea. The thing didn't want to let up but tormented me without relief. I would be freezing cold one minute, and ten blankets could not keep me warm. Then I would be so hot I had to throw off all the blankets. My body felt like it was ready to give up.

I found myself angry at God. I was all alone and I thought of everything I could have in life if I survived this. Still single, I reminded myself that I hoped to have a marriage one day. I thought of my Mom's amazing home-cooked meals. But nothing was appealing enough to make me want to live. I wanted to die. I felt that I was being pushed beyond what I could bear. I shamefully shook my fist at the sky and declared to Jesus, "You don't love me!"

That day the pastors of my church came to visit me at my home. This was not an easy errand as I was in the village and the walk was far and hazardous. After I recounted to them my unvarnished feelings about the unfairness of the universe, they said to me: "We came here to comfort you. But now we need to rebuke you." The rebuke was delivered in love, and I knew that they were right. I repented.

Finally, a nurse came from the village. She put cold washcloths on my skin to cool me down enough to receive an injection. Shortly afterward, my disease disappeared. I would go on to have many more cases of malaria, including awful episodes in Kenya and Tanzania. I was acutely aware of my frailty and found myself calling out over and over to Jesus for mercy. He was always faithful to lift the disease, and in this way I learned to trust God in those awful times of suffering.

Jonah 2:22 NIV "In my distress I called to the Lord, and He answered me. From deep in the realm of the dead I called for help and you listened to my cry."

11. Derika: My Ugandan Son

On a sunny Ugandan morning I was called from my office by one of the 133 orphans residing at our "Rihanna Home," telling me to come quickly. I ran to the front of the building and down the steps to see a five-year-old boy who had just been dropped off by his mother.

The image remains imprinted on my mind to this day: Derika had bare feet, a tattered blue shirt, and dusty black shorts. His eyes protruded slightly, and he looked up at me sheepishly, extending a note in hand. In his best English, his mother had written, "Please take my boy and raise him for me. You are my only hope of him having a good life."

The Rihanna Church Home was already filled to capacity, so it seemed the only real option to adopt him into my own home. It took some time to work out the details but Derika became the youngest orphan to come live in the Busega village with me and the other boys.

There were challenges as Derika adjusted to his new family. Like any child who is used to doing as he pleases, it took discipline in addition to affection to help him understand being part of a family. This meant getting him to keep up with chores, to assist others, and to be kind to his new brothers. With such a rough start in life, it was not altogether surprising that Derika had issues --- like stubbornness. In the beginning, when he had to be disciplined, he would retort "Sifaayo!" ("I don't care!"). But in time Derika developed into a happy young man with a good spirit and love for his new family.

All this parenting stuff was new to me. A relative youth myself, and until only recently under the charge of my own parents, I had to grow up --- fast. I was now the parent. This trajectory of growth is possible through a reliance on God: "I have more insight than all my teachers, for I meditate on your statutes. I have more understanding than the elders, for I obey your precepts. I have kept my feet from every evil path so that I might obey your word" (Psalm 119: 99-101).

How often do we chafe under the discipline of the Lord? And yet, are we not all like children who need guardrails in growing towards Christ? No discipline is pleasant in the moment but yields righteousness to those who submit to its training (Hebrews 12:11). The Lord disciplines those whom he loves (Proverbs 3:11-12).

It took effort on both our parts, but Derika obtained a special place as the youngest of the crew. At first we didn't even know Derika's birthday, so after soliciting ideas from the older boys, we decided as a family to give him the same birthday as mine. The first year of celebration, he ate so many sweets that he threw up --- another lesson learned. We would continue to celebrate our mutual birthdays together every year that I remained there. Derika reminisced to me later that he remembers feeling like the wealthiest kid ever, because he was one of the few who was given a coin to buy food for school; all the others had nothing or would bring something from home.

Derika was finally able to come to the United States, and discovered that he enjoyed the work of being a trucker. He lived in the truck and drove day and night as much as possible, saving money. In time he married a Ugandan woman who represented Uganda in the basketball Olympics, and she, too, learned to drive a truck. He would drive while she slept, and she drove at night while he slept.

When the housing market cratered in the early 2000s, Derika bought a beautiful house in a nice suburb of Atlanta. He and his dear wife are the parents of four boys and raise their children to live for the Lord. What an amazing testimony of what God can do!

I myself bought some acres of land in Ntenjeru, Uganda, a few years ago, with the intention of building missionary housing for short and moderate-term missionaries. This structure has recently been completed. In the course of the project, it was discovered that adjacent to the property I purchased lives --- guess who --- Derika's mother!

Psalm 119:105 NIV "Your word is a lamp for my feet, a light on my path."

12. Diodi and His Fat Chicken

Dereka had a dear friend his age named Diodi (the Ugandan form of David) Musitwa. David had parents, but he was one of so many children that his parents were glad for him to live with us if I would take him in. Since it made Dereka happy, we let him join our household.

We had a mid-week house church at the Busega Home, which grew to about 100 people. My only concern was we had mostly women and children. I had hoped some of the men in the village would get converted, and when I gave 'alter calls' at the end of each meeting, I was praying I would see a man or two raise his hand to receive Christ.

One week, when I was offering the opportunity to receive Christ, David raised his hand as high as he could reach. I did not acknowledge him right away as I looked around to see if a man or two might show interest. But David started making grunting sounds like 'Please recognize me! I want salvation!' I finally acknowledged him and it was so clear by his life that David had received Christ that day! He was filled with joy and peace, and his face seemed radiant.

The day finally approached that I was to leave Uganda, after 3 years living there. David wanted to give me a going away present, and he told his 'brothers' he was going to give me one of his three chickens. The one he chose was his biggest and plumpest chicken, and his brothers tried to discourage him from doing that. "Daddy Steve will be gone, and you will only have your two smaller chickens! You should give him a small one and keep the fat one." David shook his head and said, "No! I want to give Daddy Steve my BEST!" Which he did. I was so humbled by his gift, and all I could do was to accept it in the spirit it was given. His heart was overflowing with thanksgiving for his stay at Busega's home and for me introducing him to Jesus Christ!

This type of giving that David did reminds me of the story of the woman with two coins in Luke 21. It says that she gave more than she could afford. I have often been reminded by the poorest of people, what true gratitude is. They will give me a meal, when they themselves don't know where tomorrow's food will come from. In ministry we need to remember that we need to worry only about today's needs and not try to live for tomorrow. Like in Exodus 16, we need to do as Moses instructed and only pick up enough manna for today. For what we store up here on earth will be eaten by the worms and grow moldy. God provides what we need. When we need more, he will provide more. We just need to show up to collect his blessings.

Years later, I visited, and David was living in Mombasa, Kenya. He heard I was coming to Uganda, so he traveled 300 miles from Mombasa to Kampala to see me. When he saw me, he picked me up by my buttocks and hugged me with all his might. He was a very thin man picking up a much bigger man in me, and yet his love gave him strength that clearly came from his love for Jesus.

Luke 21:3 NIV “Truly I tell you,” he said, “this poor widow has put in more than all the others.”

13. Eno Uganda: Part 2

"Culture shock," they call it. Landing in a new country halfway across the world. Different languages. Different sense of what is normal. Everything we have deemed normal in life until now is not so normal anymore.

Some of your cultural faux pas may be overlooked by the new host country because people understand you are a foreigner and still getting adjusted. If you use the wrong word in greeting, this is not problematic.

But other missteps may have life-and-death consequences.

Though there was almost an absence of car traffic back when I first arrived in The Pearl of Africa, today the big cities of Kampala, Jinja, Entebbe, and even smaller towns, especially in the southern half of the country, are bustling with traffic. It was the English who introduced vehicular traffic to Uganda, and so you drive on the left hand side of the road instead of the right.

There are many who travel on foot as well, and then there are the "boda bodas." These are glorified dirt bikes used as quick taxis. They weave in and out of traffic with no real rules. Pedestrians have to watch out for these boda bodas as for any other vehicle: it is not the car's responsibility to avoid hitting you; it is your job to stay out of the way.... I mean, this is Uganda.

After planting our first church in Kampala, Jack Miller had introduced the "Back to God" crusades as a way of spreading the Gospel while meeting people where they were. As we had done in Philadelphia, we hit the streets to preach about Jesus. Street evangelism worked well, and churches were added quickly. These crusades would be instrumental in building congregations in the PCU across the nation. They began in Kampala and branched out to Jinja, Mukono, Embali, and many other areas.

After church one Sunday, my job was to use the painting company's vehicle to carry the speakers and instruments to the location of the afternoon outreach, where we were going to preach and witness. I had unloaded all the equipment at the site, and I started off back to the church to transport the choir to the site of the crusade.

As I pulled out, one of my friends called for me to stop. I noticed a strange twinge of something in his voice, and I came to a halt. I got out, and my eyes slowly focused on three men standing upright. They were holding AK-47 machine guns. I kept walking towards them, and they cocked their weapons. (Talk about culture shock.) I stopped in my tracks, and much went through my mind: in a second those bullets would penetrate my chest and I was going to die.

Long moments passed and nothing happened. The men with the machine guns seemed to take forever to decide whether to shoot me. Later, I found out that they were looking for a white man who had done something wrong. Normally, they would shoot first and ask questions later, but by God's mercy they debated and then instructed me to lie in the dirt. I lay there next to one of my close friends, feeling so much safer on the ground. My suit was dirty, but I was relieved. Peace came over me. I whispered to my friend, "Eno Uganda."

The culture of God has its own culture shock, its own strange ways to get used to. It says things like that we cannot serve two masters --- money and God. It says that what is highly esteemed among men is an abomination in the sight of God. (Luke 16:13-15). It says that I am saved by an alien righteousness and not my own, by Another's blood and not my own blood.

Luke 16:15 NIV "He said to them, 'You are the ones who justify yourselves in the eyes of others, but God knows your hearts. What people value highly is detestable in God's eyes.'"

14. Let it Snow!

Growing up in the northeast United States, snow was a regular wintertime occurrence which I absolutely loved! One of the reasons was that school might get canceled and I could enjoy a day of fun with friends and play in the freshly laid coat of white snow.

As a young person I would intently listen to our local radio KYW on those snowing mornings in great anticipation of our school number, 365, being announced for closure, or at least delay.

Living in Uganda, where temperatures rarely drop below 55 degrees Fahrenheit, even at night, I found myself really missing snow, especially as December and January rolled around. Being away from home can make you homesick in a variety of ways. It's not just missing your family; it is missing the day to day normality of a bygone life. The changing of seasons and their moods back in America never happened in equatorial Uganda, which has a rainy season and dry season but an annual sameness of temperatures.

In Uganda the leaves never changed colors and fell. The newness of spring buddings on trees, and the plants coming back to their springtime fullness, never happened. I prayed often to the Lord that a miracle might happen and somehow I could see snow in Uganda. I knew that was impossible, but I smiled and put in that request before Him.

We need to remember that the earth doesn't control God, and neither does science. "Is anything too difficult or too wonderful for the Lord?" (Genesis 18:14a). It is God who created both, and therefore it is God who is in control of both (along with everything else, of course). Job 37:6 expresses this exact sentiment: "He says to the snow, 'Fall on the earth,' and to the rain shower, 'Be a mighty downpour." In Psalm 148: 8 we read about "lightning and hail, snow and clouds, stormy winds that do his bidding."

One day I was all alone and repeated my prayer for snow. At that very moment I felt peace, and a familiar feeling in the air came over me, and a familiar smell. It was the harbinger of snow. Out of nowhere, hail started coming down --- first a few balls, then hundreds, and then thousands of pellets! It was bouncing all over the grounds, to the point that there was a full layer of hail covering all the grass and roads!

As it says in Psalm 19:1, "The heavens declare the glory of God; the skies proclaim the work of His hands." I laughed and could barely contain my amazement. God had heard my prayer. He gave me snow, or something very much resembling snow, in a country not known for snow except in the mountains, and where temperatures hung in the 80s. What a joy that was to me. And the Lord let it happen a second time the following year.

God truly cares about the details of the lives of his children.

Psalm 19:1 NIV "The heavens declare the glory of God; the skies proclaim the work of His hands."

15. Let it Rain!

When it rains in Uganda, it is absolutely drenching. When I first arrived in the country, almost all the roads were composed of compacted red clay, especially in the villages. Driving on this muddy surface was similar to driving on ice. The wheels have nothing to grip on, and one can easily slide across the lane into a ditch. These ditches are often many feet deep and would land your vehicle in a repair shop.

Rain was dangerous. It often washed out the entire road and made travel impossible in places. Today there are more paved roads in Uganda, but if you are curious to experience the conditions I describe above, just venture out to the villages and you will be sure to find them.

Rain is essential in an agricultural economy like Uganda. That's why in spite of the difficulty it presents to travel, rain is admired and looked forward to. And when it rains, it pours! There are seasons when the sky will empty itself out for days on end. But these may be followed by long dry periods, and then the crop-life suffers. So many people in Uganda live off the land and are dependent on it for their crops that during the long, parched stretches, one might do almost anything to have it rain.

Our dependence on God should be the same. Isaiah 58:11 says, "The Lord will guide you always; He will satisfy your needs in s sun-scorched land and will strengthen your frame. You will be like a well-watered garden, like a spring whose waters never fail."

During one of my many return trips to Uganda, after my early years, I was asked to give a sermon at church. A long introduction was given by my pastor Edward, and finally I walked up to the pulpit. It had not rained in almost three full months, and everything was bone dry. But as I opened my Bible to preach, dark clouds gathered in the sky. As I began to speak, rain started to come down. And it came down hard.

It was almost scary, as I could barely hear myself speak for the racket of the rain hitting the metal roof of the church, and the winds whistling through the open windows and doors. My pastor in the front row leaned forward and said, “Keep preaching!” I kept preaching, and it kept pouring.

Finally, I closed my Bible when my sermon was complete. The rain stopped. I sat down, and everyone was smiling. “Man of blessing,” they said after the service. “Will you come back and preach tomorrow?” I smiled at the Lord’s timing. The rest of the week it rained some every day.

I know I did not cause the rain; it was the power of God. Through that same divine power, Elijah had experienced the opposite phenomenon: he had prayed that it would not rain, and it didn’t. “He earnestly prayed that it would not rain, and it did not rain on the land for three and a half years.”

Elijah, we are told, was "a man just like us" (James 5:17). But when a mere man steps out in faith in a great God, interesting things happen. The infinitely powerful God hears our small voice, knows our needs, and sees our hearts.

God gave to me and the church a special gift that day.

Isaiah 58:11 NIV "The Lord will guide you always; He will satisfy your needs in a sun-scorched land and will strengthen your frame. You will be like a well-watered garden, like a spring whose waters never fail."

16. Near-Death Experiences

Stepping out is really stepping in --- stepping into the unknown. When we step out of our comfort zone, we step into the zone of dependence. In the case of Christianity, that dependence is on God. The life of entrusting oneself to one's Maker is encapsulated in Proverbs 3:5-6: "Trust in the Lord with all your heart, and lean not on your own understanding; in all your ways acknowledge Him, and He shall direct your paths."

In the early days in Uganda, my close American friend Alan would insist that "the safest place is in God's will." I have had many years to reflect on that saying, and I can honestly say that Alan was correct.

I mention this because anyone stepping out in faith is faced with the pull of the flesh that tries to convince you that it is safer to stay home and in a place you know. It was only through many near-death experiences that I learned to rely on God.

The day before my first trip to Uganda, I was driving late at night and fell asleep going down a steep hill. I woke up near the bottom and saw I was heading straight for a telephone pole. I frantically turned the steering wheel, missing the pole by a few feet, and ending up in a ditch. As I lay there, the song on my tape player was James Ward singing, "Consider the lilies how they grow. Your heavenly Father takes control. Are you not much more important than they? What can your worry do anyway? Seek first the Kingdom."

A tow truck appeared out of nowhere and pulled me out. The next morning I couldn't believe how my car looked. I shouldn't have survived the crash. Or at least I should have been injured. God was sending me a message of assurance: He would be with me on this trip to Uganda.

In another incident, my orphans and I were driving to school, and we came to a "Y" on the road. It was my habit at junctures like this to ask them which way we should go. On this particular day they chose to go to the right. As we started to turn down the right side of the fork, a bomb blew up on the left fork, the route we could just as easily have taken. Coincidence? God's angels protect those in His will.

Years later, I was heading back to Uganda, and there were threats of bombings to happen on July 4th in Brussels (where I fly through) and in Mukono in Eastern Uganda, where I was heading. I paused to consider what I should do. I chose to stick with my plan despite the speculations. As it turned out, while I was in Uganda, a bomb did blow up --- but it was in Chattanooga, five minutes from my house in the USA! A week after I returned to Chattanooga, a bomb blew up in Brussels at the exact place where I had been two weeks before, near the luggage claim I always passed!

Once, I was going for a walk in Chattanooga on my birthday. A group of men pulled up and told me to get in the car. They brought out a gun and started putting bullets in it. They told me their dad was part of the Black Mafia and that he could kill a person and the police would leave him alone. I explained to them that I understood a lot of what they go through as minorities. After 45 minutes they let me out. I told them to feel free to visit me again, and I turned into my home. As I exited the car I thought they might shoot me while I walked away. They didn't shoot, and they didn't come back either.

It seems a man is unkillable unless God decrees otherwise.

Romans 8:38, 39 NIV "For I am convinced that neither death nor life, neither angels nor demons, neither the present nor the future, nor any powers, neither any height nor depth, nor anything else in all creation, will be able to separate us from the love of God that is in Christ Jesus our Lord."

17. Lead Me Away From Temptation

Billy Graham had a personal rule to never travel alone. He was wise. 1 Corinthians says, "If we want to know the Lord and become more like him we must surround ourselves with friends who desire the same things." Whether alone or with someone, I found a strong need to pray the 'Lord's Prayer' every day. I learned from the Ugandans to pray that prayer: "Lead us not into temptation but deliver us from evil."

Matthew 6 and Luke 11 both make the point that we need to pray in this way. Why does God stress this so much with us? Because spiritual warfare is a daily battle. Ephesians 6:10 warns of this battle; we must put on the full armor of God, being strong in the Lord and only in this way can we resist the devil and his attempts to lure us away from righteous behavior. When we are following God and going out into the world to preach the Gospel, these attacks may come even more often, and with less warning and blatancy.

Once, I had traveled to Uganda for a funeral, back to the USA for one day, and then to Senegal, West Africa. I was exhausted and had just preached. As I lay down to take a nap, an attractive lady speaking broken English approached me wearing a very skimpy outfit. She alerted me, "I will come back tomorrow." I was immobile. I had no strength and was very susceptible to temptation. I told my traveling companion we must stick together from now on, but I did not tell him what happened.

The next morning, we were having devotions together, and this lady returned. This time in pink underwear and a see-through outfit. When she saw my friend there, she stopped in her tracks and left the room. My friend did not know what had just happened and then I explained it to him.

In Kenya, I was traveling with a friend. At the end of a long day, we pulled into a small hotel, and both sat on our two beds and had left the door open a crack. I looked up, and there was a woman sitting next to me and one sitting next to him. How quickly they came into prey on our exhaustion from travels and our natural weaknesses as men. I told them to leave, but again, I was taken by surprise and maybe if I had traveled alone and my friend wasn't there, who knows what would have happened.

In Uganda, we would have "night prayers" which began at 6 pm, and since there was a curfew till 6 am, the prayer time would go on all night, and we would walk back to our homes. One night after prayer, I was walking home, and one of the ladies from the night prayer invited me to stop by for coffee. When we got to her home, she started to hold me and her face became 'longing looking.' I felt pulled by her, and not in a good way. It took all I had to push her off me and get out of her house. It was another 'close call,' and only by God's mercy did I avoid this temptation.

Pray the Lord's prayer every day alone and with other believers. Keep in mind that none of us are immune from the pulls of the evil one, but with the help of the Holy Spirit, we can resist temptations.

1 Corinthians 10:13 NIV “No temptation has overtaken you except what is common to mankind. And God is faithful; he will not let you be tempted beyond what you can bear. But when you are tempted, he will also provide a way out so that you can endure it.”

18. Aortic Dissection

In 2008, I was traveling with a young pastor to Uganda to help him catch a vision of what the Lord was doing there. I hoped he would adopt Uganda as one of the projects his church would involve themselves in. David liked what he saw and was excited to participate in some way in the days to come.

I asked David if he would travel home alone so that I could stay behind in Uganda another week or so, but he humbly asked me to escort him back to the U.S., as he had little traveling experience and would feel better with me accompanying him. I chose to do that, and this decision saved my life.

We arrived home safely, but I had picked up a case of malaria and was vomiting violently the first two days home. The next day I went to church, and most people said that I did not look well.

The next morning, I was planning on driving to New York on business, but when I started my day I had an awful pain in my body and knew that things were not normal. I whispered to my kids, "Please get Mom." My wife called the ambulance, and I was rushed to the hospital.

Initially the hospital was going to treat me for a stroke. This treatment would have thinned my blood in order to prevent it from clotting --- which would have killed me. My blood pressure had suddenly dropped beforehand, which was confusing. The doctors then did a full body scan and found that my aorta was filled up with blood and was about to burst.

I was rushed into surgery under the care of two highly skilled surgeons. They told my family to phone anyone who might want to say goodbye, as it was not likely that I would survive. They gave me a 4% chance to live and to be fully-functioning. They surgically removed my heart, putting me on a bypass machine to circulate blood through my body. They placed my heart on ice and cut the valve to it, replacing it with a fake piece that was developed by the army. The operation went well. For rest and recovery, they placed me in a coma so that my body could heal and wake up slowly.

On the fourth day of my induced coma, the doctors said to my family that if I did not wake up within the next 24 hours, I would likely be in a vegetative state the rest of my life.

My wife thought to herself, "Who do I know who believes in healing?" She remembered Faith Fellowship International (FFIC), a church committed to Five-Fold Ministry, and who believe that God can even raise people from the dead. When she called them they responded, "We have been waiting for your call." They had been doing a prayer walk for me every day since they had heard of my hospitalization. Being a patient congregation, they had waited to be invited to the hospital.

The people from FFIC arrived and laid hands on me, anointing me with oil. Even though I had tubes in my mouth and my eyes were closed, I watched the whole proceedings from "the other side," and still can picture them to this day. During the operation I had flatlined on the table. So what the Lord did through FFIC was nothing short of miraculous.

That same day I woke up and was able to walk around! The prayer of righteous people had spared my life (James 5:14-16). I got up and went around praying for others on the floor, a unit of the hospital that was reserved for patients in the worst of conditions.

One man I prayed for had a heart operating at only 30%. I told him what had just happened to me and asked if I could pray for him. He could only nod his head "yes," as tears ran down his face. Six weeks later, I saw him at my fitness club on the treadmill, three machines down from me. God had restored him to full health.

At a follow-up visit post-recovery, I met with my doctor and he said, "Every doctor has one or two cases that they refer to as their miracle case. You are mine." God raised me up completely, and now, sixteen years later, I am still doing the work the Lord called me to in East Africa.

Philippians 4:6, 7 NIV "Do not be anxious about anything, but in every situation, by prayer and petition, with thanksgiving, present your requests to God. And the peace of God, which transcends all understanding, will guard your hearts and your minds in Christ Jesus."

James 5:16b NIV "The prayer of a righteous person is powerful and effective."

1 Peter 2:24b NIV "By his wounds (stripes) you have been healed."

19. That's My Trash!

Being a missionary can be challenging, but I imagine it is especially so in the case of Americans. Going across cultures is probably hard for anyone. But coming from the "greatest country in the world" to living in a country recovering from civil war can fray the nerves.

Nothing is ever normal. And yet to be effective, one must adapt to one's surroundings and learn the other's culture. One must be in control of oneself and learn to smile when one feels like screaming. One must hold his tongue when sneered at or laughed at or when one mispronounces words or struggles with tasks that are simple for the native. Pride was often an issue for me on the field, and I became upset when people were scornful of me. Proverbs 17:27, 28 exhorts us to exercise restraint, warning that if we do not, we will look like fools.

Westerners are also a bit more private and have a strong sense of ownership: "What is mine is mine, and what is yours is yours." An unwritten rule in the West is that you should not invade my space or touch my things. In Uganda this is much different. Life is a shared experience there. Nothing is considered off-limits from use, and "borrowing" from someone is a common practice.

Back at home in the U.S., I was used to having a trash can in my room or office. I looked far and wide in the little shops of Uganda, and it was nearly impossible to find something that resembled a trash can.

Finally, I came upon a basket that looked like it would do, brought it home and started to use it.

Within a day or so, one of my orphans wandered into my room and started to take things out of my trash can, to see if he could make use of it. My reaction was embarrassing and shameful. My nerves frayed from no sleep after the all-night prayer meetings of the weekend, and still frustrated at how long it had taken me to find a basket that would serve as a trash can, I yelled at the child, "That's my trash! Leave it alone! If I call something trash, it is trash!"

The dear boy looked at me with hurt eyes; he had never meant to cause harm. In Uganda people make use of just about everything. Rarely is anything thrown away as trash. Even loose sheets of used paper can be repurposed as toilet paper.

I look back on that scene and realize how much I need a Savior. Here I was, trying to be a man-of-God missionary, and instead I was a spoiled white man who resented anyone touching anything I owned, including my trash.

Proverbs 17:27, 28 NIV "The one who has knowledge uses words with restraint, and whoever has understanding is even-tempered. Even fools are thought wise if they keep silent, and discerning if they hold their tongues."

20. Garbage Truck Evangelism

Rev. Kefa Sempangi: Church visionary and gov't official. He arranged to get a garbage truck for us to use during our evangelism outreaches, and provided the Busega home with a soldier to protect us during this turbulent war time.

In those early days post-Amin, there were few operational public services. Electricity was rare and there were rolling blackouts throughout the country. Some days you would have it, then suddenly you would not, and you would never know when it would return.

And this was just in the cities, which were the more fortunate parts of the country! As for the villages, even to this day they do not have electricity in their homes. There is no public water service for 99% of the country. All the available water is rainwater collected into tanks.

Post-Amin there was also no public transportation, such as buses and subways.

Which leads me to trash collection. Trash trucks had not been in use for over a year. Most trash, which mainly consisted of banana peels and other organics, was piled up in small mountains throughout the land. The stench from the gaseous output of degrading material made for unpleasant commutes on the street.

Jack Miller and Harvey Conn came up with a creative idea. We would "kill two birds with one stone" --- clean up the trash and share the good news of Jesus Christ at the same time. This definitely wasn't an ideal job, but helping the community seemed an effective way to share the Gospel.

We asked the government if they would loan us one of their trash trucks. They obliged because we had a friend in the government (the refugee and seminarian Kefa Sempangi mentioned in an earlier chapter) who put in a good word for us. Besides, what government official in this new post-war era wouldn't jump at the chance to garner good will from the community for the small price of loaning out an unused trash truck?

The plan was that with our newly acquired government refuse collection vehicle, some of us would venture into neighborhoods and remove undesirable waste. Meanwhile, one or two of us would preach the saving grace of the Gospel, and how through repentance God is able to clean up the garbage in our lives. Perfect, right?

We told people that cleanness and righteousness from God was freely given to anyone who would repent and turn his life over to Him in obedience. Though the content of our hearts be like trash (or as "filthy rags," as the prophet Isaiah put it), God would transform them.

There was a man who had committed multiple murders , who was overcome by the grace of the Gospel during one of our trash talks. At first he was infuriated and intended to kill the speaker, my friend Bob Heppe. He approached the place where Bob was preaching, looking for an opportunity to attack. But before Bob had finished his public appeal, the man's heart was transformed by the words of life. He ended up joining the team of evangelists.

Nearly a thousand people in all raised their hands to receive Christ under this unique evangelism outreach. (Not to mention that twenty large piles of trash were collected off the streets of Kampala!)

Isaiah 64:6 NIV "All of us have become like one who is unclean, and all our righteous acts are like filthy rags; we all shrivel up like a leaf, and like the wind our sins sweep us away."

21. That Looks Delicious!

Most of us have probably not experienced the type of hunger that leads us to thievery. Proverbs 6:30,31 says that we are not to despise a man who steals in hunger, and yet there is still a consequence if he is caught. We all have been hungry in the West, but most of the time we are able to find food rather than resorting to stealing from someone else. When we do steal in a first world country, it is generally out of wanting rather than actual needing.

The Presbyterian Church of Uganda Painting Company mostly painted government buildings and international companies like gas and oil depots. But we also took on some jobs painting the houses of the few rich people who lived in Kololo near the capital city of Kampala. Kololo has some very nice western-style homes which only a few can afford.

One day our painting company was working for a wealthy Ugandan in that town. The owner came home and was served a cold beer by his servant. He began reading his paper as I was on his veranda painting white columns. The servant proceeded to bring him a plate with a delicious looking steak, along with nice vegetables and an Irish potato. My mouth watered for that meal, and I began remembering the meals my Mom used to prepare back in my homeland.

Mom was a renowned cook. All my friends wanted to be invited to our house for one of her famous Greek dishes. Mom would serve a six-course meal and apologize as she brought each course out for not having made the other dishes she knew we liked.

This Ugandan homeowner finished his meal but left one chunk of meat on the plate. I wanted that meat and would give anything to get it. The servant came and cleared the table and took the plate and utensils out to the kitchen. I slowly painted the baseboards leading to the kitchen, and when no one was looking, I snuck into the kitchen and grabbed that meat!

This incident of being famished, and sneaking a partially eaten piece of leftover meat off a foreigner's plate, is the epitome of hitting bottom on the mission field. I had stooped to the level of stealing food from a servant's mouth. If I just stayed where I was, I would be able to have steak for dinner every night if I wanted. Lord have mercy!

What about you? What would you give for a morsel of food?

Genesis 25:32-34 NIV "'Look, I am about to die,' Esau said. 'What good is the birthright to me?' But Jacob said, 'Swear to me first.' So he swore an oath to him, selling his birthright to Jacob. Then Jacob gave Esau some bread and some lentil stew. He ate and drank, and then got up and left."

Matthew 6:13 NIV "And lead us not into temptation, but deliver us from the evil one."

James 1:13 NIV "When tempted, no one should say, 'God is tempting me.'"

22. Rose Marie

Like this Cape Buffalo, Rose Marie was full of quiet strength as she walked alongside her visionary husband, Jack Miller.

Being married to someone called to the mission field is not easy. The missionary's focus is on the work of ministry, and often a spouse feels left out, or overwhelmed with shouldering a greater burden of the household.

Of course our first responsibility is to our own household: "Anyone who does not provide for…their own household has denied the faith and is worse than an unbeliever" (1 Timothy 5:8). But for the missionary whose face is set like flint on doing God's work, there are many households to look after. It can be challenging for a couple yoked in the service of God.

Rose Marie Miller knew that challenge, as the wife of the visionary Jack Miller. It is Jack who convinced all of us to go to Uganda back in 1980. This was a time of particular stress in politically unstable Uganda, as its government had already been overthrown three times since Idi Amin was deposed in 1979. But Jack had a passion for the spread of the Gospel, whatever the cost. And Rose Marie, as his devoted wife, accepted to be his helpmate, not just by letting him go to Africa, but by stepping out with him into the unknown.

One night, while our team was in Uganda, we had an overnight prayer meeting at Jack and Rose Marie's house in Rubaga. That night gunfire and missiles filled the skies. Guerrillas were trying to bomb the police and army barracks nearby. The bombardment came so close that we not only heard and saw it but felt it too.

On the floor we lay in fear for our lives --- pastors, elders, women, young recruit missionaries, and a few children. The insurgence went on all night, and sleep was not an option. But God was with us, and we knew that even in death nothing could separate us from his love (Romans 8:38,39).

God had mercy on our lives, and with the coming of morning the attacks ceased. I was then sitting with Rose Marie and I could tell she was emotionally spent. She had been faithful to the work, but this close call pushed her to the limit. In the quietness after our brush with death, she and I talked about the daily challenges of the work --- the effort it takes to adapt to another culture; the need to leave behind one's comforts and desires; the constant vigilance required against theft or violence; the constant need to forgive.

Rose Marie leaned on my shoulder and, right then and there, called out to the Lord for help and strength to carry on with the mission. As 1 Peter commands us, she cast all her cares on God, committing herself anew into His safe hands. She knew He was her only hope to stay the course.

And the Lord did renew her strength, and she continued to be a huge blessing, not only to her husband, but to all of us. Rose Marie's spirit energized and inspired the rest of the team members and many others in the First Presbyterian Church of Uganda.

Isaiah 40: 30,31 NIV "Even youths grow tired and weary, and young men stumble and fall; but those who hope in the Lord will renew their strength. They will soar on wings like eagles; they will run and not grow weary, they will walk and not be faint."

1 Peter 5:7 NIV "Cast all your anxiety on him because he cares for you."

Dr. Jack and RoseMarie Miller

23. "Things Don't Have to be This Way!"

Have you ever been in a position where you knew that if people just cared for each other the outcome would be so much better? We live in a selfish and shattered world.

Psalm 34:18 reminds us that "the Lord is close to the brokenhearted and saves those who are crushed in spirit." As missionaries we see many who are brokenhearted and crushed in spirit --- the eyes of the mother of a starving child; the destitution of those who lack even the basics of life.

One fellow American I spent a great deal of time with in Uganda was Alan. He was a deep thinker, you could almost say cerebral. Despite differences in age (he was a bit older than me) and experience, we were fond of each other and went through many harrowing adventures together. Alan would always try to process our experiences in the light of God's Word, and the Holy Spirit gave him insight.

The trip to Uganda cost Alan a lot. During his stay, from May of 1980 till January of 1981, the distance from home and lack of ability to communicate with people there took a toll on his relationship with a woman he had contemplated marrying. But he never took his eye off what God asked him to do in ministering to the Ugandans, who were in much need of the Gospel.

Because of the curfew of those days and the intermittent electricity, when darkness fell there was nothing to do but talk to each other by the candle's dim flicker. Alan and I talked about everything, including the disintegration of his relationship with the woman he loved, and the real possibility that in the dangerous societal conditions of post-Amin Uganda, we may never return to the United States.

During the national unrest, many took justice into their own hands. If a thief was caught, you would find a mob dragging him to the police station, but on the way administering a vigilante justice that was worse than his sentence and incarceration would be, beating him and tearing his clothes off.

Life was almost surreal around us. Hospitals --- if they could be called that --- were unsanitary. Their toilets were no longer working and were filled with human waste. How could someone be healed in a place like that? Scenes like this were enough to eventually drive even a composed and even-tempered person like my friend Alan to cry out in exasperation: "Things don't have to be this way!" He was done trying to make sense of it all.

God knew the desires of Alan's heart. Within nine months of returning home, he got engaged and married. He and his wife would go on to have three sons. The eldest joined his father on a work trip to Uganda. And later, both this son and the second oldest went again for a six to eight-week program for college students with Christ's School.

Deuteronomy 31:28 NIV "Assemble before me all the elders of your tribes and all your officials, so that I can speak these words in their hearing and call the heavens and the earth to testify against them."

1 Chronicles 28:20 NIV "David also said to Solomon his son, 'Be strong and courageous, and do the work. Do not be afraid or discouraged, for the Lord God, my God, is with you. He will not fail you or forsake you until all the work for the service of the temple of the Lord is finished.'"

24. Junior Partners and Those We Serve

Many years ago, my father was head of a non-profit called 'Partnership in Missions.' My Dad was convinced that working with organizations and leaders in developing countries must be a partnership. Certainly not a dictatorship, and ideally in such a way that the indigenous leadership would be affirmed as they lead, and in such a way that those leaders would grow and develop to their potential. For this to happen, my father was convinced we westerners need to not only view these relationships as a partnership, but additionally, we would discipline ourselves to be junior partners!

By design, and for the long-term health of the local indigenous community, we need to consciously have the Spirit of John the Baptist. Jesus' cousin once said, "I must decrease, and he must increase" (John 3:30). It is not easy for us westerners to "be slow to speak, quick to listen, and slow to anger" (James 1:19). It is natural for us to want to assert ourselves. The people we serve may even desire us to take over and we must hold back so that God can do His work. We have many ideas we may attribute as great, from living in an advanced country like America. We will believe we move the growth ahead by dominating many of the conversations and sharing stories of how we learned and what our experiences have taught us.

On several fronts this somewhat innocent tendency to assert ourselves helps us with our agenda, but it does not develop leadership and decision-making skills. The leadership of the church we are working with tends to be silent and politely tends to shake their heads with the hopes of not offending us, because they may feel that if they reject our ideas then we will reject them or leave.

Sometimes I see our visceral control as relatively innocent. If we examine this behavior closely, we can come to a determination that this is really a cultural character flaw on our parts. I remember when a very talented individual who knew how to build wells was preparing to go to Uganda. I listened to his language, and it was very clear; he had a plan and he had goals, and he fully intended to put a couple hundred wells into existence for the health of the local churches and their people.

A few months later, I was with him in Uganda talking at one of our church gatherings. One of the pastor's wives came to greet my friend in the typical Ugandan way, gently interrupting our conversation to curtsey and respectfully greet us. My friend was almost agitated by her interruption and seemed oblivious to the cultural greeting even though he had been in Uganda for almost a year. Clearly, he was highly motivated to make a difference, yet he had not made any real connections to the people he was there to serve. My friend could almost be described as a "bull in a china shop." He was very frustrated with the people and honestly felt he wasn't appreciated by those he was serving.

The reality was that this man had no interest in hearing the priorities of the local leadership. He never asked them for their opinions, and his frustration ended up turning into criticism. This tendency by us westerners is very common and very natural. I remember being criticized by my Ugandan pastor that I did not take time to greet the widows who did much sewing each day in front of the church. He said I offended everyone by waving a quick 'good morning' as I headed into my church office. I too was critical initially and thought to myself that 'half their problems are most likely that everyone is sitting around doing nothing!' It is so easy for us to judge coming from a country of smooth roads, healthy food, free education, and much more. We simply don't get why these developing countries are so broken. Once an American shouted out to me, "These people have all the resources we have available to us in the USA! There is no reason things should be so broken down!" Undoubtedly, he had very little patience for the effects of rogue political leadership, famines, corruption, and much more that can disable a nation. I had to apologize to this visitor, as I believe I offended him by trying to get him to see things as those we serve, see them. He was not ready for that perspective.

An organization in Chattanooga, Tennessee called 'The Chalmers Institute' has a book called *When Helping Hurts*. It points to some of these realities. That we may be trying to help people in need, and we often bypass the church leadership and give directly to the people. On more than one occasion, I gave resources to the leadership in Uganda and the church members never received the goods. It is very easy for me to conclude it was a mistake not simply giving it to those I could clearly see were in need. But the truth of the matter is that the leaders of God's church need to be lovingly held accountable and be shown the scriptures where leaders are to be shepherds to their flocks. To "feed my sheep" as Jesus said in John 21:17. I started to take the pastors on retreats and share some of these thoughts as we ate and enjoyed some peace away from the demands of the ministry. I have continued to do these retreats for the past 40 plus years. The leadership of the local churches needs to be strengthened by us junior partners.

Years ago, my father was part of a stateside Uganda committee. He suggested the unthinkable; to have a Ugandan on a Ugandan committee! A novel idea, wouldn't you agree? It simply is very difficult for us who have years of experience and success to go to a developing country and play second fiddle. For the sake of the long-term health of the church we serve, we need to cultivate a spirit of humility and a spirit of John the Baptist, placing ourselves as the servant, so that the Gospel can be spread and so that Jesus can work in the hearts of the people, and we can see leadership growth amongst them. All of this is to be done to the glory of God and his church!

John 3:30 NIV "He must increase, but I must decrease."

Mark 8:35 KJV "For whosoever will save his life shall lose it; but whosoever loses his life for my sake and the gospel's, the same shall save it."

25. Divisions, Church Splits and Personality Conflicts

Years ago, I was a junior high youth leader at my church in the States. Our church befriended a primarily African American congregation. Our youth groups would have joint events, including playing miniature golf.

One night after playing golf, we went out for ice cream. Some of the other patrons of "Rita's" (a Philly water ice chain) seemed surprised at how young black and white teenagers could laugh and enjoy one another's company. One bystander, seeing I was part of this group, asked me what was going on. I told him that we were from two local churches in Glenside, and that the junior highers loved the Lord, and that was mostly what united them.

When I was still a young Christian, God planted John 17 deep in my spirit. The passage describes the heart of God. It shares the deepest wish of Jesus as expressed in his prayer to his Father, a prayer often referred to as Jesus' "Priestly Prayer." Here Jesus pleads, "May they be one, as we are one." Jesus wanted us to experience the powerful sensation of true unity.

But there is more. Jesus discloses an additional purpose of oneness: "So the world will see and believe." Why will the world believe if they see our unity? I think it is because unity requires selfless behavior. Unity requires laying down one's life for others. It involves denying oneself, and being slow to speak, quick to listen, and slow to anger --- all things that are not naturally found in the world but only supernaturally found and therefore evidence of God in us.

It is amazing that all it takes to stand out at a water ice road stand is two sets of kids with different ethnicities but the spirit of friendship, sharing a summer snack. It is enough to make the world stand up and take notice.

Equally noticeable, but in a negative way, are incidents where people of faith have disagreements that lead to separation. Such break-ups in fellowship also bring attention to the Church and leave those watching disillusioned, which is not the heart of our heavenly Father. The devil delights, for he roams around seeking victims to devour. If he can get believers to devour themselves and each other, all he has to do is sit back and relax as we do the work for him.

Leaders of my church came up with the idea of starting self-help small businesses to support the work being done in Uganda; these would employ the locals to whom we were bringing the Gospel. It was a wonderful and unusual approach, as most mission agencies at that time would only preach the Gospel in "word"; very few ventured into outreaches geared to meeting physical needs as well as spiritual needs.

I was too young at the time to sit in on the meetings where the Ugandans and Americans met to plan and discuss. I speak therefore as a bystander, and cannot say precisely what happened in those meetings.

What I do know is that, somehow, very well-intended and godly leaders came to an impasse in those conversations, resulting in sharp division between the two groups. After all the battles we had fought together to reach the lost of Uganda, a decision was made to go our separate ways. We had gotten tripped up in disunity, and this brought a short-term blemish on Christ's Church.

Nor was it just the Americans and Ugandans who split up. There arose division within the Ugandan leadership as well. This began with a pastor falling into temptation. Half the leadership said he must be removed not only from leadership but also from attending worship services; the other side disagreed. Both sides had good reasons for their convictions, and maybe division was necessary. But we all must be on the watch for how easily we can fall into a trap. As Paul exclaimed in rebuke: "Is it possible that there is nobody among you wise enough to judge a dispute between believers!" (1 Corinthians 6:5). The Apostle continued that when we parade our disputes and dirty laundry before the watching world we are "completely defeated already" (v.7).

Other splits took place over doctrine. The original church plant back in 1980 was founded on Reformed theology within Presbyterianism. Two of the pastors eventually decided that Presbyterians were too somber, and they chose to leave the original church plant and start Pentecostal churches. Again, this may have been the only option, for there are times when division is actually necessary

(1 Corinthians 11:19), but I did notice that pastors who before the division used to enjoy each other's company at sporting events no longer had any interaction after the split.

I know of a case where one leader of the mission team inadvertently made a casual (but unnecessary) statement. It could have been overlooked (Proverbs 19:11 says it is "a man's glory to overlook an offense"). But one of the field workers took great offense, and the next things you know the whole mission team was rife with tension. The ministry ended up undermined, and onlookers watched in disbelief. How had it all started? James 4:1-10 tells us what causes divisions --- our passions, wrong motives, and unbridled tongues.

I have seen occasions when a member of a team is critical or inconsiderate of others. This happened as early as our exploratory team. It led to grumbling, as people didn't want to be around him. And this not only affected the team locally, but word got back to the United States, and rumors spread. "A little leaven spreads through the whole lump." That in turn makes it hard to convince churches and individuals at home to see the mission work positively and to want to support it.

We must be on our guard against the world, the flesh, and the devil, "in order that Satan might not outwit us. For we are not unaware of his schemes" (2 Corinthians 2:11). We must be diligent to keep the unity of believers "so that the world may see and believe."

John 17:23 NIV "I in them and you in me --- so that they may be brought to complete unity. Then the world will know that you sent me and have loved them even as you have loved me."

1 Peter 3:8 NIV "Finally, all of you, be like-minded, be sympathetic, love one another, be compassionate and humble."

26. Snakes, Cockroaches, and Things That Move at Night

Fear can be the biggest obstacle in a ministry. It stops us from moving forward even though it may be irrational. Have you ever seen a little kid so afraid of a small insect that he will throw a fit until someone smashes it? Other fears may be considered reasonable: fear of a lion or bear standing within feet of you, for instance, or fear of speaking before a large crowd.

The Lord understands men's fear and addresses it. When commanding Moses' successor Joshua to march into Canaan and conquer it, He said to him: "Have I not commanded you? Be strong and courageous. Do not be frightened, and do not be dismayed, for the Lord your God is with you wherever you go" (Joshua 1:9).

I faced many fears in Uganda but my biggest fears may surprise you. One was Bugs.

Even prior to entering Uganda, I have always found the thought of insects in the house, lurking near the places where I slept or ate, unsettling. Would it surprise you that one of the unpleasant by-products of civil war such as in Uganda --- besides the understandable scarcity of resources and damage to families --- is increased menace by the lower species of nature?

God himself attests to the danger that disruption or upheaval of the animal kingdom poses to man during times of warfare or civil instability. He says this to the Israelites as they embark on conquest of Canaan:

"I will not drive [the Canaanites] all out before you in one year, lest the land become desolate and the wild animals multiply against you" (Exodus 23:29; Deuteronomy 7:22, 23).

The first house I lived in had cockroaches everywhere. I could hear them as I tried to sleep, and when I turned on a light, they scurried all around me. In an attempt to assure myself a good night's sleep, I did a thorough cleaning of every inch of the house.

My second house had huge rats. The only other place I ever found rats that large was at a restaurant in Kampala. Rats are disgusting creatures, roaming wherever they please with little fear. Again I did a very thorough cleaning of the house until it was finally rat-free.

One time I woke up with a snake under my pillow! But what would have been unheard of in my home in the states was a common occurrence for the orphans I cared for. Undaunted, they came into my bedroom and drove the vermin out, saving the day.

In the villages the comfort of a mattress was unusual. Often your bed was made of layers of large banana leaves. I once spent the night on one of these makeshift beds in a rural village. Crickets had somehow gotten trapped in the layers beneath me and had no way out. They sang that song that crickets do by rubbing their legs together. As there was no light in the village at night, I could not take my bed apart to try to release the trapped insects, and so I was serenaded to sleep that night by a cricket concert.

My co-worker Bob and I were relaxing on the side of a road one evening when we suddenly heard what sounded like a rattlesnake in the grass next to us. We had no idea if rattlesnakes were native to the area, but we didn't want to find out the hard way. If we had been bitten, there would have been little chance that a hospital could help us in war-torn Uganda. We made a quick exit.

Another time, when Bob and I were rooming together, in the middle of the night there was a shrill noise that sounded like a huge tiger cat. We were both petrified, but neither of us knew the other had heard it. We didn't move all night, and the next morning the incident was the main topic of conversation.

But there lurked worse dangers and fear for me than the animal kingdom, dangers I had not anticipated. A bigger challenge for me than the subhuman world was the world of human relationships. Relationships among team members and relations with the nationals proved harder than dealing with multi-legged creatures. This is because I am a sinner, working with other sinners. I should have expected interpersonal issues.

People often would intrude on my space, and my tendency to irritability would come to the surface. Our fellow missionaries felt violated when people would touch our pockets and say things like "Praise God, brother Steve, I am hungry." Yet didn't people do the same to Jesus? Wasn't there a woman who touched his robe, and didn't He respond with compassion, "Daughter, your faith has made you well; go in peace" (Luke 8:48)?

Daily being put on the spot to decide if we should invite a stranger into our private world took a toll. For a while, I wanted to put the people we were serving aside at 6 p.m., as if they were my day job, and to return to my home and retreat to my private world with a "Do not disturb" sign on the door.

Over time, God's Spirit convicted me of selfishness. He helped me to submit to the local church leadership, and to be quick to repent when I had a wrong attitude or was short-tempered. I often felt like I was the only one apologizing, but that's okay because I was in their world, and that is a privilege not to be taken for granted. The Ugandans had let me into their world; it was I who was afraid to let them into mine. Perhaps I feared seeing too much of myself. Perhaps I feared exposing my hidden thoughts of being better than them, or my sense of privilege, or my lack of dependence on God.

As challenging as it was on many fronts, those first three years in Uganda were seasons of growth for me, whether by facing the lower species or fellow men. This was the period, more than any other phase of my life to this day, when I became more Christlike. Stepping out, even when you are afraid, pays dividends not only for those you serve but for yourself. This is true whether yours is a short-term mission trip or embarking on full-time service.

Though sometimes unnerving and fear-producing, missions are an adrenaline trip well worth taking. There is nothing like seeing the Gospel spread and the hand of God at work, in my own heart and in the hearts of those He has sent me to serve.

Proverbs 9:10 NIV "The fear of the Lord is the beginning of wisdom, and knowledge of the Holy One is understanding."

Philippians 4:6, 7 NIV "Do not be anxious about anything, but in every situation, by prayer and petition, with thanksgiving, present your requests to God."

27. July 4th

Being a missionary doesn't mean being perfect. Peter lost faith that God could keep him afloat (Matthew 14:22-33), and later denied Jesus three times after the last supper (Luke 22:54-62). The disciples all lost faith when their boat was caught in the storm, and they woke Jesus, blaming Him for not caring (Mark 4:35-41).

John and the other apostles didn't realize God's power went beyond their inner circle, so they rebuked the man who cast out demons in Jesus' name but who was not in their group (Luke 9:49,50). The twelve often failed to realize who Christ really was, and the purpose of His ministry. They often were caught up in the world, rather than in the spirit of Christ.

July 4th is a special commemorative holiday for Americans, celebrating our independence. One year, on this day, I, along with two other Americans, went to the U.S. Embassy, where there was a special event which provided us with the familiarity of home. We were treated to hotdogs with relish, mustard, and ketchup, and cotton candy for dessert, things we hadn't enjoyed in what seemed ages. It was a great day.

Afterwards we went back to the house of one of my friends to play board games, and somehow we got a hold of a bottle of whiskey. We nursed the bottle of alcohol while Bob's wife (Bob was at Buvuma Islands preaching the Gospel with other pastors) joined us for a game of Monopoly. We ended up drinking the whole bottle. The next morning brought me a hangover and my spirit was downtrodden.

I went to visit my good friend Franz in the industrial center, and when he saw me in that sorry state, he closed the door and told me to get on my knees with him. He told me to pray and give it to God. He knew that was the best answer for his Christian friend, even though he himself wasn't yet a believer! He knew this was not the "real" Steve, and couldn't stand to see me so not myself.

I asked the Lord to forgive me for my un-Christlike behavior, and came to grips with the reality that I must be vigilant to "walk in a manner worthy of the calling" (Ephesians 4:1). The man of God cannot take days off from being a man of God, even if it is the fourth of July.

We all make mistakes, even when we are ministering. We must be careful of these things, though, as the face of God is represented by our actions that people see. When we do sin, falling short of the calling, we must be humble and repent, "so that times of refreshing may come from the presence of the Lord" (Acts 3:19).

It will not only be the good deeds we do that people see, but also our reliance on Christ for our salvation and forgiveness of our indiscretions. Likewise, we must be ready to lift our brothers and sisters up when they fail, not holding these failings against them, but rather coming alongside them to guide them back to Christ. Ephesians 4:3

instructs that we need to "make every effort to keep the unity of the Spirit through the bond of peace," because each of us has been given grace. What a God we serve, who loves us even in our depravity.

Acts 3:19 "Repent, then, and turn to God, so that your sins may be wiped out, and that times of refreshing may come from the Lord."

Ephesians 4:1, 2 NIV "As a prisoner for the Lord, then, I urge you to live a life worthy of the calling you have received. Be completely humble and gentle; be patient, bearing with one another in love."

28. Where is the Church?

The church we planted in 1980 was growing by leaps and bounds. That body of believers kept sending out saints who had matured as Christians, dispatching them to the four corners of Uganda. Often I was included in those outreaches and came in contact with dear people who were in extreme spiritual and physical poverty.

Have you ever seen a belly so full of worms, yet so empty, because the person hasn't eaten a thing for many days? Have you seen a child with a wound that is literally eating away at his flesh, while flies and gnats try to take their turn to gain some nutrition and a place to lay their eggs?

Matthew 25:31-46 reveals the fate of those who look after the needy, versus those who pass by without seeing them, or seeing them, avoid them. This present chapter is meant as a wake-up call, not a guilt trip. I must quickly remind myself of how often I have looked past obvious ways I could have served someone in need, and did not. If today I more often seek to help those in hardship, it is only by the grace of the Lord. And only the Lord can judge us.

One of the outreach leaders asked us to share the gospel in the area he grew up in in eastern Uganda, near Lake Victoria. This was a fishing village, and many of the men who came to fish would stay for weeks at a time, trying to make money. They would stay in small makeshift huts.

Local women and girls, destitute of resources, would take advantage of the desires of men, and prostitute themselves for a meal. This behavior led to the spread of disease. The men would then bring back disease to their village and spread it to their families and to the community. Locally known as “Slims,” the disease is what we know as AIDS (Acquired Immunodeficiency Syndrome), and it spread rampantly throughout Uganda in the 1980s.

I stood on a hillside in the village of Ntanzi, with two great leaders of the Presbyterian Church of Uganda, Kefa Sempangi and Edward Kasaija. We looked out over the eleven villages of the Ntenjeru sub-county that could be seen from this spot. All of these people within the scope of our vision were people who had needs that were unmet. Many of them had lost hope. Many had not yet heard the gospel, had not been introduced to their Creator and Savior.

The village of Mpunge that we had been asked to visit had over 3,000 people awaiting our arrival. They pressed in against me, clamoring to show me their medical prescription slips. The slips all said “Tylenol.” The answer given to their AIDS epidemic was some sup-optimal pain medication to ease the pain until they passed away. I was the only white person there, and looked at this mass of humanity crying out for help. I wondered to myself, “Where is the Church?” I wondered if the thousands of dear Christians in the USA had any idea of what is out here. If they knew they would come, right?

A year or so later, I brought a well-seasoned philanthropist to that village. She had been to India and many other developing countries, yet she said to me that she had never seen such poverty in all her travels. The church leadership in Uganda had gotten the call and saw the needs of these people, but could only meet a small number of the physical needs.

I kept thinking that we Christians are the salt of the earth. We are the hands and feet of Jesus. How can we as a Western church society, privileged in so many ways, ignore such broken people in need of the hope of the gospel? The church was MIA!

One day I returned from the village of Mpunge and went back to my room alone. I had kept a hopeful face before all the people I had been with in the past twelve hours, but inside I was hurting for these people. When I got behind closed doors I began to weep. I held my chest with my hands because it felt like it was about to burst. I tried to figure out whom I could call on back home to help.

Three days after I returned to the United States following these visits to Mpunge for the first time, I had my aortic dissection (see Chapter 18). One Christian doctor I knew said he could see that my heart had been broken in Africa. I never asked what he meant, I just took it in. The pressure on my heart from witnessing the broken village of Mpunge hit so hard that I believe it caused my aorta to rupture.

We cannot continue to ignore such a great need. When the Church is "missing in action," the people we fail to reach become "missing in heaven." Many of the stories I have shared in this book are about personal sacrifice. This one is about love: do we love people enough to make the gospel known to them? Is their sin any greater than ours? We need to think about this question individually, but there needs to be an awakening in the Church. The gospel is not meant for only some but rather as the answer for all men, who are "lost, without God, and without hope" (Ephesians 2:12).

Matthew 25:40 NIV "Truly I tell you, whatever you did for one of the least of these brothers or sisters of mine, you did for me."

Matthew 9:35 NIV "The harvest is plentiful, but the laborers are few. Pray to the Lord of the harvest to send more laborers."

Mark 16:15 NIV "Go into all the world and preach the gospel, making disciples…"

29. My Third Tattoo

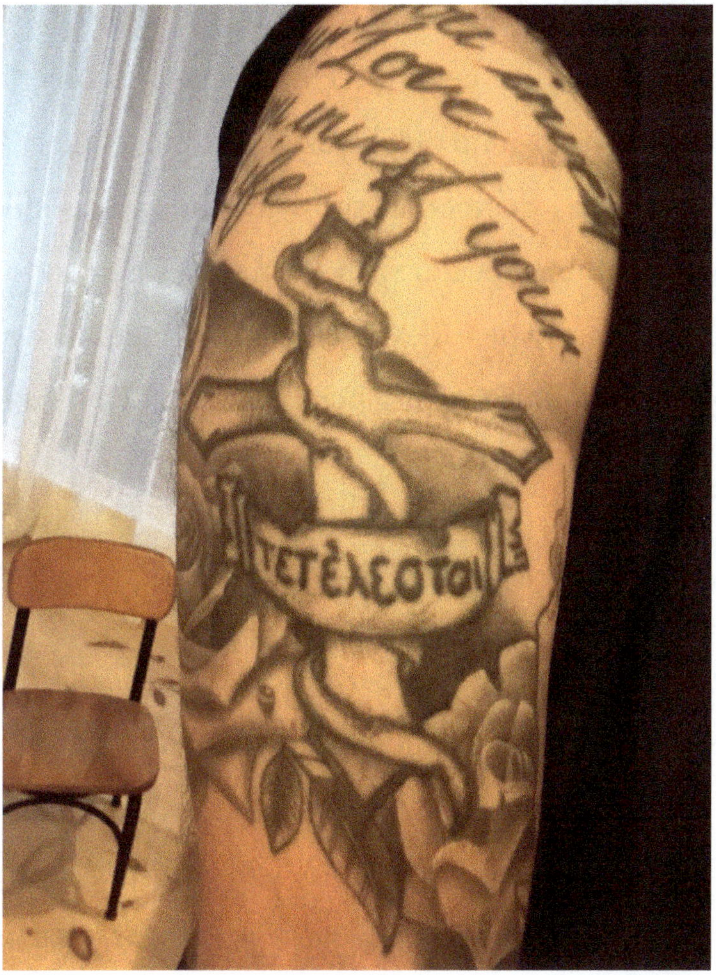

Your legacy is a gift you leave behind for those that remain after you. In the end it defines who you were. The parable of the talents, in Matthew 25:14-30, reiterates that we are given gifts in this world by God. It's what we do with those gifts that is important to God. God doesn't just want us to return to Him. He wants us to add to the number of Christians on earth by investing in the people around us. One of those gifts is family, and more specifically for me, was my wife and the children we have raised.

At the turn of the century, tattoos had become increasingly popular. It seemed young and old, black and white, male or female were all getting "tats" and I decided to show the kids I was still relevant. I wanted to do something special with them, and I agreed to get a tattoo with all three of them when they each came of age. A way to signify their passage into adulthood, yet a bond that would still connect us.

I would choose a Bible verse that would reside on my skin the rest of my days on earth. The verses would be important words from God that I did not want to forget. My oldest, Mike, was obviously the first one I was able to have this experience with. I chose Ephesians 3:20, to remind us of how powerful and omnipotent our God was, is, and will be. This verse had been my favorite verse from the time of my conversion at the age of seventeen. Mike was in the Army and we shared this moment at a shop near his base in Arizona. He chose an American flag, symbolizing the importance of his service to the country that provided it with freedom and protection. My right shoulder continues to hold this verse and the memory of this bonding moment lives on, even though my son has passed on before me. Leviticus law implies that even our skin belongs to the Lord. The marking on my skin is a permanent record of the power of the living God, who I continue to believe will do big things if I follow Him.

As my daughter came to the same pivotal point in life, the ascent of adulthood, I again embarked on this symbolization of connection with both my gift from God and our Savior. Stacy had fought through many battles that could have easily taken her life. At two weeks old my wife and I watched our daughter fight for her life with encephalitis. A few years later, she accidentally ran through a glass door and the glass cut through her throat. But nothing ever kept Stacy from fighting. She never saw something as impossible. She even made the men's college soccer team as a starter. Her voracity on the soccer field played out just as much, in the rest of her life. She decided on Joshua 1:9, her life verse to be written out on her shoulder. Stacy is fearless in many ways, and these words of God would remind her that he would be with her always. This reiterates His commitment to her and encourages her to be strong and courageous in the Lord and to 'fear not,' which has been her motto and conviction throughout her life to date.

My tattoo choice was Philippians 4:13. This verse is surrounded by a map of Africa, with the countries of Uganda and Senegal highlighted in red. These were two areas where I had special work going on in ministry. I felt that God was using me and strengthening me to spread the Gospel in these often-forgotten places. Looking back, even though I had good intentions, I ask myself: Had this focus pulled me too far away from the ministry of my family that God had given me, as a talent to invest in for His glory?

My son Matthew was the last to reach adulthood. He is very artistic and creative, like his mother, and he designed his own tattoo. It was three arrows representing himself and his two siblings. Two arrows were pointing in one direction towards a finish line and the other arrow, representing his late brother Mike, was pointing in the other direction, because he had finished his race already. His sister, Stacy, got this same design in solidarity with her brother.

When it came to my last tattoo, I chose John 21:15. In this verse Jesus commands Peter to "Feed my sheep." The shepherding of God's sheep, I believe, is one of the greatest honors and charges that Jesus makes. "Go and make disciples of all nations" (Matthew 28:18)." This is the greatest way for us to show God our love for Him: By loving each other and having compassion on those in need. I strongly believe that if more of us had that Christ-like conviction and compassion for others, we would draw so many to the Kingdom.

Even ministry can be taken to an extreme. My sensitive and intuitive daughter had ministered with me locally, in nursing homes and to the homeless in the city of Philadelphia. She also served as far away as Japan, Uganda and Tanzania. She respectfully spoke to me regarding my choice of verses for my third tattoo. "Dad, honestly, you don't need any tattoos reminding you to feed Jesus' sheep. What you really need is a tattoo that says, 'remember you have a wife and three children who need you to be home more and who need you to lead the family in a God-honoring way.' You have done enough ministry for one lifetime Dad! You need to minister to your family, while you still have them under your roof."

Wow! She was right. I rationalized all the time away from my family as serving the Kingdom of God, and all the while, I was not honoring my first calling as a husband and father. My life was out of balance and it took my dear daughter to point that out.

My family and kids needed to know their importance to me, like the importance God sees about all people. My family had members who were really struggling, and I was more focused on my ministry abroad, than caring for them. My third tattoo reminded me that, in the process of trying to live out a radical following of Christ, I failed to keep my commitment to honor and cherish my wife, and I failed to fully show my three children that they are precious to God as seen by the love of their earthly father.

This is a very important lesson for any of us well-meaning disciples of Jesus as we step out in ministry. We must remember our first ministry, which is the gifts God has betrothed on us in our own home. As Psalms 127:3 says, “children are a heritage from the Lord” and Proverbs 18:22 reminds us that “He who finds a wife finds what is good and receives favor from the Lord.” Maybe one of these will be my next tattoo, but I need to make sure, whether these are on my skin or not, that they are embedded in my heart. As I seek to serve the kingdom of God, I need to devote time to the talents he has given me, so that when he returns, I can account for how I invested the gift of the family he gave me, while also going out into the world to spread the Good News.

Matthew 28:19 NIV “Therefore go and make disciples of all nations, baptizing them in the name of the Father and of the Son and of the Holy Spirit.”

Matthew 25:21 NIV “His master replied, ‘Well done, good and faithful servant! You have been faithful with a few things; I will put you in charge of many things. Come and share your master’s happiness!’”

30. Train Wreck: God Will Provide

The Busega home where twelve orphans and I lived for two years was a happy place. Everyone had responsibilities which, although not always desired, were necessary in order to have our daily essentials met and to succeed.

Chores included fetching four "Jerry cans" of water from the well, cleaning up the yard and house, and making sure daily homework was completed and ready to submit to teachers the next day.

We made sure to include an equal amount of fun into the schedule. After school each day we had a family sports time, and following a warm dinner (usually of beans and "matooke," a local plantain-like fruit that when cooked and mashed resembled the yellow pastiness of mashed Irish potatoes), we would sing worship songs and share testimonies of how God had provided for us.

Another activity the kids and I looked forward to was my custom of visiting each of the orphans' home villages, clans, and family members, in rotation. The orphans loved parading through their old stomping grounds and pointing out all the things they remembered from early childhood. They were proud to introduce me to their remaining family members, and we were able to spend time talking and eating together.

Some of these trips were a good distance from the village of Busega. One particular village, Tororo, was a few hundred miles away, and you needed to take a train for several hours, then hope to catch a passing vehicle that would be going deep into the village where my "son" Peter Tumweiseje came from.

When we arrived, we were greeted with open arms and welcomed by his extended family. Although most families were happy to see their young relatives, you never knew exactly what to expect. Peter's relatives exceeded our expectations, preparing a "cozy" bed for each of us, fashioned of banana leaves stacked several inches off the ground. They fed us to our hearts' content.

After a few nights of rest and enjoying the company of Peter's family, he and I headed back home with our arms full of live chickens, fruits, and vegetables, parting gifts to take back to our orphan household. We found our way out of the village to connect with the train, and in due time boarded for our journey. About three hours into the trip, in the middle of nowhere, the train somehow derailed. I say "somehow," but in Uganda, especially at that time, nothing was surprising. The familiar sick feeling of uncertainty came upon us. There was no way to send a message home, so all our pressing domestic responsibilities would have to be put on hold.

The two of us disembarked and watched as passengers started to use up the stored water available outside the train. They were washing themselves in it, with no thought of conserving the limited amount. I knew we could be in trouble if the train did not get repaired soon. We were truly in the wilderness, far from stores or houses or any place to get help. We reminded ourselves that God was with us wherever we go, and that He is our guide and strength (Psalm 139:10).

Many of the stranded passengers were drinking the local banana beer as we all waited in the hot sun. We had some food, but no way to cook it. In order to get it cooked we were forced to give up half of what we had to a person who had the means to cook the food. As we needed to eat, that was the best deal available.

By the third day, our food supply was used up, many of the passengers had become unruly, and we could only pray for God to provide a way back home. Somehow, by day's end the train was put back on the track and we were on our way without further incident. At long last we reunited with the other orphans, who had been worried by our delayed return.

As we reflected on Philippians 1:6, it was clear that "He who began a good work in us" had kept us from all harm and granted us safe passage to our Busega Homestead. When we do the Lord's work, which includes honoring these children's life stories as important, God knows how to find a way where there is no way.

Adventures such as these happened with regularity. Unpredictability became the only thing predictable. When God asked Abraham to sacrifice his son of promise, Abraham imagined the most humanly unpredictable scenario --- that if Isaac died, God was able to raise him from the dead again (Hebrews 11:19). Which metaphorically

He did. Our forefather spoke in faith when he said, "God Himself will provide the lamb for the burnt offering, my son" (Genesis 22:8).

We never know when we will be stranded or faced with mini crises where we have to call out to God for help. How wonderful is the life of total dependence on God. When we take the adventure of faith, it joins us in spirit to Abraham, Noah, Moses, Mary, Joseph, and others of the cloud of witnesses.

Genesis 22:8 NIV "Abraham answered, 'God Himself will provide the lamb for the burnt offering, my son.' And the two of them went on together."

Philippians 1:6 NIV "Being confident of this, that He who began a good work in you will carry it on to completion until the day of Christ Jesus."

31. Guilty as Charged

Have you ever been caught in the act? We make mistakes in life. Sometimes these mistakes are intentional, as when our desires take over. Sometimes these mistakes are not intentional; we just lack the wisdom to realize that what we are doing is offensive. Either way, all have sinned and "fall short of the glory of God" (Romans 3:23).

As I stepped out in faith to serve God in the country of Uganda, I knew that I wanted to see change happen. I wanted to make a difference. I knew this would take hard work and determination. After all, I was about to go to a country where the dictator had killed so many people that the burial grounds could not contain them.

Each day I set out to find ways that could improve the lives of the people of Uganda. I strategized business plans, I worked on where to get food and clothing for the orphans under my care, and for others as well. But though I labored day in and day out, things did not change readily. I wanted to make a good impression and to prove myself worthy of being regarded as a change agent, but my motives often came under scrutiny, and I was often scolded for my abrupt conduct with people.

Most days I would start by waving to the widows sitting in front of the church knitting as I entered my office. I thought this was a pretty good way to greet people and to show that I was friendly and I cared. What I learned is that I was viewed as rude and unkind. Uganda is a country where relationships are valued highly. I was falling short of the

Ugandan cultural view of relationship, as I was not taking the time to greet each lady one at a time.

I couldn't believe it! Here I was working to help them. Who has time to stop and just talk to each of them. I mean some days there were many of them sitting there. They had all the time in the world, as they didn't have jobs or husbands. Someone like that could pass the time of day chatting, but I had a mission to complete.

As we transplant ourselves into a foreign country, especially one not suffused with Western influence for many years, we need to remember that all that we say and do are under a microscope. Many of the Ugandans have never seen a "Muzungu" ("Westerner," or, informally, "white person") in their lives. Like it or not, I would be a representative of all Muzungus for these, in my words and deeds.

My American pastor, Jack Miller, would often quip, "Cheer up! You're worse than you think you are!" His point was that we should stop defending ourselves and stop trying to act like we don't need a Savior. He believed that God knows us better than anyone, and He sees all our shortcomings, yet he died for all of it. We don't have to be defensive; we just have to put our trust in the finished work of Jesus Christ on Calvary.

Seeing these women just sitting there knitting on the steps of the church, my first instinct was to mumble to myself, "That's half their problem! They're sitting around doing nothing instead of hustling and fixing some of the problems around here. And besides, I know that my motive is to make a difference, and they are wrong to judge me so harshly!" The reality, of course, is that the problems of Uganda didn't happen overnight, and they won't get fixed overnight by one or two zealous missionaries.

Even if the women had misjudged me in this particular case, the truth is that there are many other ways in which I sinned that they had no knowledge about, but that God saw and knew. And we know from James that "whoever keeps the whole law but stumbles at one point is guilty of all" (James 2:10).

Several times I had soldiers' guns trained on me, and I realized that even then I was not humble. Moreover, how often I had granted myself the best that was available in terms of food and clothes. Yet if I had died there in Uganda, people in the West would have hailed me as a special and courageous person, which would have been far from the truth. The truth was that I was a chief sinner, saved solely by the mercy of our Lord.

I found myself convicted about my over-sensitivity, and about the high opinion I had had of myself, imagining myself to be a gift to Uganda. I had fallen into the trap of self-importance, of being more concerned with how I was viewed and how I would be remembered. This is the trap of the Pharisees, who "loved human praise more than the praise from God" (John 12:43). Brother James points to the way out of this moral morass: "Humble yourselves before the Lord, and He will lift you up" (James 4:10).

The easiest thing in the world is to want to defend yourself. Add to that natural fleshly tendency the emotional edginess produced by living in an underdeveloped country, and you have a perfect storm. The lack of a warm shower, three meals, and a soft bugless place to lay one's head will quickly bring the aspiring missionary face to face with his own human frailties. He might well ask himself, like Paul, "Who is equal to such a task?" (2 Corinthians 2:16).

The answer is that it is God who makes us equal to the task, but not without a constant dependence on Him in prayer. Otherwise we build nothing of lasting value. If we vainly imagine we will straighten everything that's crooked in Uganda in our own flesh, we are like the fool described in Psalm 127:1,2: "Unless the Lord builds the house, the builders labor in vain. Unless the Lord watches over the city, the guards stand watch in vain. In vain you rise early and stay up late…."

It is God who will build His house. Ours is to present ourselves as His humble instrument, and nothing more.

James 4:10 NIV "Humble yourselves before the Lord, and He will lift you up."

Romans 3:22b-24 NIV “There is no difference between Jew and Gentile, for all have sinned and fall short of the glory of God.”

32. What We Do in Life, Will Echo into Eternity!

For kids the first introduction to the concept of infinity is mind-boggling. The character Buzz Lightyear of the children's movie *Toy Story* uses the infamous line, "To infinity and beyond!" According to the Bible, from the moment we are conceived, we are destined to exist infinitely. Christ died that we might have eternal life (John 3:16), but it is sobering to remember also that those who are not of God "will be tormented day and night, forever and ever" (Revelation 20:10b).

In the film *Gladiators* Russel Crowe stars as Maximus, a true warrior of valor and integrity. The commander of the Armies of the North under the Roman Empire inspires a huge military force to go to their deaths, if necessary, for the greater good of Rome. His stirring speech and demonstrated bravery are what galvanize a ragtag unit of loyal fighters to victory over the German barbarians.

As we go out into the world to make disciples of Christ (Mark 16:15) let us encourage one another that the battle is not ours but the Lord's, and He will go with us wherever He leads. Stepping into the fray is risking life and limb, as it was for Maximus against the German hordes. But our stepping out emboldens others who will come after us to step out. That is, our actions here on earth ripple through eternity, "to infinity and beyond."

In my travels I visited a missionary family in London. The father and mother were longtime friends of mine, and whenever I came to town, we would have a wonderful time of fellowship. I was passing through London after a month in Uganda visiting many of the Busega orphans, now grown men, as well as some of the men from the church painting company I helped start.

As I sat at the table with my friends in London, I shared with their children how satisfying it was for me to meet the wives and children of the painters and orphans so many years later. What joy it was to see the smiles and joy of these African brethren, to hear them share how blessed they were to have grown up in the orphan home, or to have been trained in our paint company. The painters remembered so many details of the things I taught them --- about drips and how to protect items that are not to be painted, and much more. My Busega boys remembered not only the fun times, but the discipline they had received, and how that discipline had led them into the right path.

I was warmed to the depths of my soul to know that my sacrifices of American life, comfort, security, foods, et cetera, were all worth it.

I looked at my friends' children in London, who were roughly the age I had been when I first went to Africa, and said, "What things are you putting your hands to today that will bear fruit thirty years from now?" One of the children was not walking with the Lord at that time, but a couple years later he did come to know the Lord, and ended up moving to India and working to help former prostitutes. He married a local girl there, and has established a home for himself there doing ministry full time.

The battles that Maximus won were great, but the battle you and I are engaged in is not for the soul of a country but the soul of every individual, who will exist forever, either in heaven or hell. The stakes of our actions are eternal. This is why God warns so severely:

"When I say to the wicked person, 'You will surely die,' and you do not warn them or speak out to dissuade them from their evil ways in order to save their life, that wicked person will die for their sin --- and I will hold you accountable for their blood" (Ezekiel 3:18).

But "Christ's love compels us" (2 Corinthians 5:14) to bring the gospel. "The one who is wise saves lives" (Proverbs 11:30). "Whoever turns a sinner from the error of his way will save him from death and cover a multitude of sins" (James 5:20).

Marcus Aurelius, Emperor of Rome, is credited with saying, "What you do now echoes into eternity. So use your power." The sooner you get on board and start planting forever seeds, the greater the joy you will experience seeing eternity being affected. Be open to letting God use you to affect the outcome of eternity.

Matthew 28:19,20 NIV "Therefore go and make disciples of all nations, baptizing them in the name of the Father and of the Son and of the Holy Spirit, and teaching them to obey everything that I have commanded you. And surely I am with you always, to the very end of the age."

Mark 16:15 NIV "Go into all the world and preach the gospel to all creation."

33. "Missionary, Go Home."

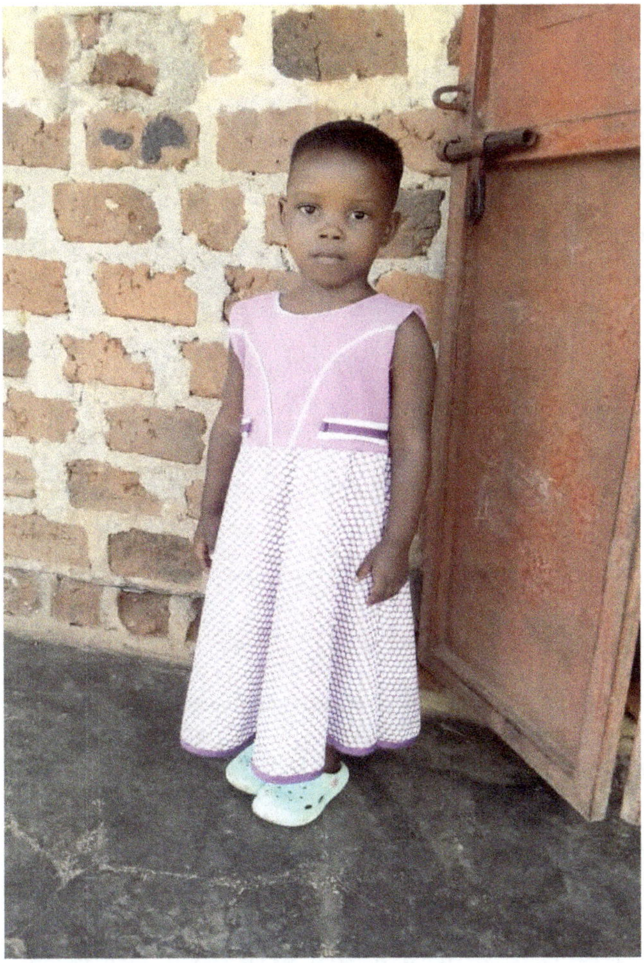

Have you ever shown up in the middle of a project and just taken over from the leader and provided the solution? How has that worked out for you?

"Missionary, go home!" These were the harsh words written by one of the pastors I worked under in Uganda. He penned a pamphlet along these lines in his intense frustration with missionaries coming to "help." These foreign "helpers" were in effect dictating to the Ugandan churches instead of listening to them and allowing them to lead.

Let's say the solution that the newcomer has offered in a church project brainstorming session is actually a good solution, and it would work. Nevertheless, the problem is that the man has usurped the rightful leader's position and demeaned him in the eyes of others. Do you think that leader will be respected by those he is leading? We Westerners too easily slip into the role of "calling the shots," and thereby unintentionally step on toes of those we came to serve.

At first the Ugandan leadership was polite and showed deference, but as time went on, they found themselves wishing the Westerners had not come. They felt the only good these Westerners had brought them was material things. They took to quoting the Tanzanian President, who said, "He who pays the piper calls the tune!" The *Muzungus* enrich the church heads materially but eviscerate them as leaders. No decisions can be made if the White man is not around. Congregational members bypass the appointed leadership and go directly to the Whites, where they know the real decision making is done.

As I write this, it seems like common sense. But the fact is that we Americans and Europeans are so used to leading that we just naturally give our opinions and start directing. And since many of the African leaders do not have the rich tradition of generations of leadership to draw on, and many lack the formal education that is a Western luxury, these local shepherds find themselves overwhelmed, and succumb to the forcefulness of the Americans.

The leadership model most familiar to Ugandans is what they see in their national politics. Ruthless dictators employ force to get the people to comply. The dictator barks out commands. Against this dark backdrop, it is important for us as missionaries to resist our natural bent and to model a pure biblical leadership whose long-term goal is to work ourselves out of a job!

Godly leadership must be the future of the developing Christian world, and godly leadership is "servant leadership." This is what we need to model as we come to foreign shores to "help." We can take a page from James, who laid out for our meditation the following qualities of the "wisdom that is from above" --- "first of all pure; then peace-loving; considerate; submissive; full of mercy and truth, and good fruit, impartial and sincere" (James 3:17).

Leaders who embody these qualities find joy in raising up men and women to become all they were meant to be in Christ's Church.

John 3:30 NIV "I must decrease and He must increase."

Matthew 20:26-28 NIV "Whoever wants to become great among you must be your servant, and whoever wants to be first must be your slave."

34. My Purple Room

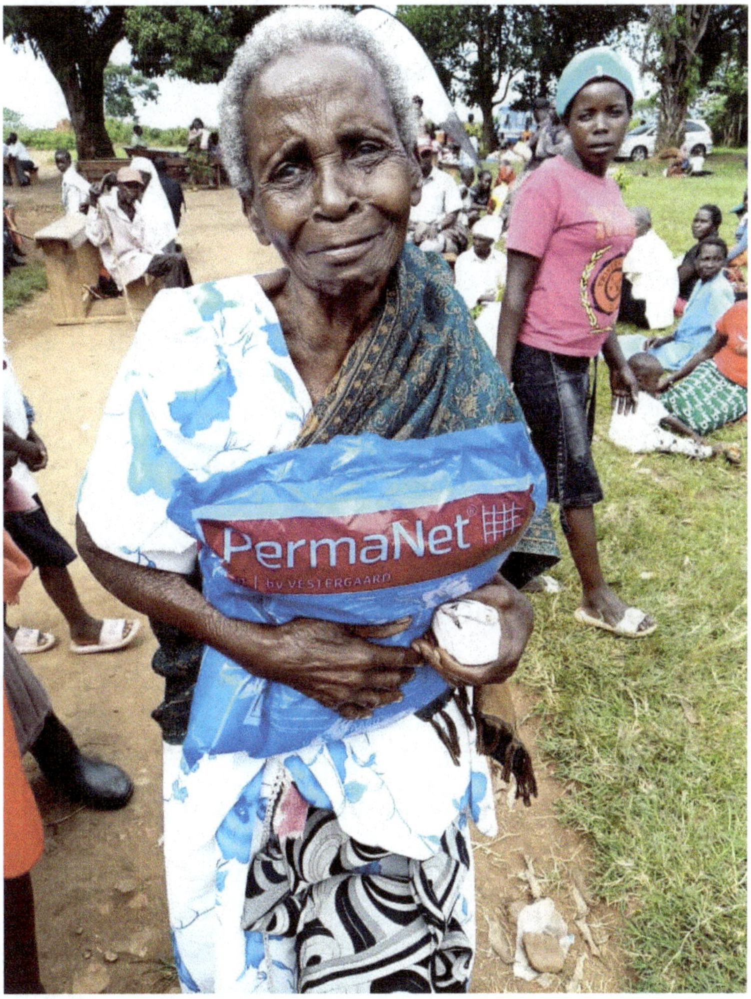

In John 16:33, Jesus gives us all a 'heads up.' He says, "In this world you will have trouble, but cheer up, I have overcome the world." He lets us all know that even as Christians, the effect of a fallen world is going to touch all of us. Whether we are laymen, pastors, elders, evangelists or missionaries, none of us are exempt from having thorns in our flesh (2 Corinthians 12:7). And the good news is that Jesus overcame the world, as he was tempted in every way yet without sin (Hebrews 4:15)! He overcame it and he is sending his Holy Spirit to help us in our weaknesses.

Over the years, I have found from experience that some 'thorns' come with sickness or diseases that don't exist in a perfect world. We do catch colds and flus and in my case in East Africa Malaria for a week at a time! Death and suffering was not God's original plan and a day is soon coming where he will make all things new! But until then, even God-fearing believers will have trouble to overcome.

There are other troubles which we bring on ourselves. In 2 Samuel 11:2, we read of the dramatic story of King David, a man after God's own heart, who chose to not go out to battle, which kings usually do in the spring. And since he was not where a king is supposed to be, he had wandering eyes and simply couldn't resist when he saw Bathsheba bathing. His decision, to not be where he knows kings ought to be, led him to multiple bad decisions. It led to broken fellowship with God his Father. It led to murder, and his behavior surely was a stain on anyone claiming to be a follower of the God of Abraham, Isaac, and Jacob. Samson and many others who were part of God's people did many noble and praiseworthy acts. But as with Nebuchadnezzar, God can humble those who walk in pride.

We all are familiar with godly leaders who were the talk of the town in one season of life. They were men or women who had great testimonies, but at some point fell into sin, for one of many self-inflicted reasons.

My dear parents always took a half hour every Saturday night to pray for all the church leaders they knew far and wide. They were very close to many leaders through my Dad's work at 'Partnership in Missions,' as well as a lifetime of being involved everywhere they went. They prayed because they knew that the devil works overtime for leaders to be tripped up by pride, lust, power, and control. It is so easy to fall into those things when members of the church do something as simple as congratulating you on a sermon you just preached. Unless a leader is walking humbly with his Maker every day, and unless he welcomes constructive criticism in his life, he or she can easily fall in love with themselves.

And other trouble can come to any of us who lead, because we take on too much. People are quick to run to the latest leader of the church, and open doors for them, to the point that they lack enough time to be still before our Creator and pray and fast and other necessary private times all leaders need.

And we also can easily slight the people closest to us. For me, I honestly thought it made sense that my family and I needed to all lay down our lives for the ministries God was leading me into. We can cause bitterness in a godly spouse when (in my case) she feels she is at best "second fiddle." And even though our children are a gift from the Lord, some leaders rationalize investing in other people's families, while our own children suffer.

This is a pitfall that I fell into. And it was not because I was trying to prove myself with my ministry work. It was that I absolutely got energized from my hours with different cultures, forms of worship, seeing people come to life, and much more. I did a form of corban (a onetime gift dedicated to the temple) like the Pharisees did in the Gospels. They declared much of their money as designated solely for God, thus excusing themselves from the commandment that the Scriptures had laid out for them to properly care for their aging parents.

As I alluded to in the chapters 'Guilty as Charged' and 'My Third Tattoo,' putting ministry at least equal to and often more than my family, eventually was harmful–especially for my wife. She really needed to be loved and cherished and courted. And if I found that a burden, I should have taken a huge step back and gotten my own life in order, before trying to change the rest of the world.

On one of my returns from Africa where I didn't even call home, my dear wife said that enough was enough. She asked me to leave. I had failed her for 39 years in terms of loving her as Christ loves the church, and she did not want to make it an even four decades.

I share this part of my life, even though it is painful to do so. But my hope is that others can learn from my failings. My benign neglect, at best, affected my wife who had told me at one point she was “head over heels” about me. She was right. I had gotten my priorities messed up, and I not only hurt my wife, but I hurt my children, and tarnished the Church of Christ! May the Lord have mercy on me, a true sinner.

I share all of that to say that I practically hit the bottom, including a season where I self-medicated using alcohol. I ended up renting a room on the third floor of a house in my hometown. A purple room!

At first this room represented me and my huge failures. It was my punishment for living a life out of balance and not being disciplined like some godly men I know, including Jack Miller and my amazing father. Surprising as it was to me, I know many near and far were praying for me. Many knew that I had God's Spirit in me, but I was like Peter and took my eyes off of Christ and His commands for me to love my wife.

Over the past year or so healing has been happening in my soul. I have no defense of my sins. I don't blame anyone except myself. I know that my sins are forgiven, and that I am loved unconditionally by my

Creator. I now see this purple room as God's love and kindness to me, a sinner in need of a mighty Savior. It has come to be a place to be still and listen to the Spirit's still small voice. Paul went to Arabia to be able to commune with God alone. This purple room has become my Arabia, where I see God teaching me, and I see myself leaning more on him and the grace he has for me. All in my purple room!

My only hope is that, like God used Paul, he will use me, a sinner who has been called by God. My hope is that my failures will spur others on to do things the way God has commanded. My hope is that, as I change, the grace of God is seen by others as He works in me. My hope is that I continue to become less and my Creator is lifted up more. My hope is that from the depths of despair, I will one day be seated at the feet of my God and that my mistakes will be forgiven and that I will see brothers and sisters all around me praising God for what he has done for us: saving us from ourselves.

Romans 8:1 NIV Therefore, there is now no condemnation for those who are in Christ Jesus.

Romans 8:35 NIV Who shall separate us from the love of Christ? Shall trouble or hardship or persecution or famine or nakedness or danger or sword?

35. The Great Commission: Matthew 28:16-20

As Jesus was leaving the disciples' world, he gave them a charge as seen in the last chapter of Matthew. We are to make Christ known–His love, His faithfulness, His mercy, His laws, and His righteousness. Our whole purpose for being on this earth is to promote the Kingdom of God by being part of his church and giving ourselves fully for Kingdom priorities including evangelism, outreach, and sacrificial living.

Matthew 19:22-24 captures the sadness of a would-be disciple who walked away from Jesus feeling very 'sorrowful' because the man's wealth was too precious to him to part with. It is a huge challenge for those of us who have known peace and affluence, to do as Jesus did. He left glory behind; he left the riches of heaven to live among us and suffer death for our salvation. It is not easy for any of us to subject ourselves to discomfort and other harsh living conditions, for the sake of bringing life to the lost. Jesus continued on in this passage, saying, "It is easier for a camel to go through the eye of a needle than for someone who is rich to enter the kingdom of God."

My experience in the developing country of Uganda is that there were many hardships and sacrifices I had to make. Yet looking back now some 40+ years later, it was so very worth it! The pain of hardships such as hunger, lack of medical help, insults from those I was trying to help, fifteen plus bouts of malaria and much, much more, was very little compared to the delights of watching the extreme joy in converts and fellow Christians whom I survived and thrived with as co-workers. I found that 'seeking first the Kingdom of God' (Matthew 6:33) truly brought me unexpected, serendipitous experiences that I never could have predicted!

So, take the promise of Jesus to heart as you step out in faith: "And everyone who has left houses or brothers or sisters or father or mother or wife or children or fields for my sake will receive a hundred times as much and will inherit eternal life" (Matthew 19:29). This has proven itself 100% accurate in my life and I am so sure it will happen for you as well if you just step out in faith, not waiting for the right moment, but rather living the moment in Jesus: our Savior and our King.

Matthew 28:16-20 NIV Then the eleven disciples went to Galilee, to the mountain where Jesus had told them to go. When they saw him, they worshiped him; but some doubted. Then Jesus came to them and said, "All authority in heaven and on earth has been given to me. Therefore go and make disciples of all nations, baptizing them in the name of the Father and of the Son and of the Holy Spirit, and teaching them to obey everything I have commanded you. And surely I am with you always, to the very end of the age."

Postscript

Lisa Sorenson, President of Word and Deed Ministries

My story is about how God designed my path to cross with a contagious missionary named Stephen DeMoss.

In the summer of 2011, my husband (also named Steve) was attending a Christian Leadership Conference in South Florida. He arrived with a request: "I am seeking prayer to hear God's plan for this sabbatical season of life." He received a prophetic answer to his request.

Steve was taking a leave of absence from work for a year. Robert DeMoss Sr., a mature Christian and friend of my husband's, said to him: "Oh, I know what you're going to do; you're going to do missionary work with my son in Uganda." Steve replied laughingly, "Oh no, I'm not a missionary, especially to a third-world country." My husband returned from the conference and shared that conversation with me. The Holy Spirit planted the seed of the idea in the back of my mind.

At that time I had just finished my BA in Ministry from Palm Beach Atlantic University, and was working part-time for a small mission organization serving Costa Rica. Several months passed after that encounter between my husband and Robert DeMoss, but I was prompted for some reason to ask Steve, "Whatever happened to that contact you mentioned, about doing mission work in Uganda?" My husband said he had never followed up in any way, other than a casual email.

I asked him for the contact information of Mr. DeMoss, so that I could introduce myself. Through several email exchanges, we arranged a meeting in Florida. Stephen DeMoss was living in Tennessee and happened to be coming to visit family in Florida, so we asked that he stop by our house.

We had a lovely visit, and I enjoyed hearing about Stephen's experiences in Uganda, initially as a college student. He shared the story of one of his pastoral relationships, Reverend Kefa Sempangi, was forced to flee Uganda during the time of dictator Idi Amin. He mentioned that Pastor Sempangi had written a book about this, and he thought I would be interested in reading it. We said our goodbyes and Stephen casually invited us to join him and his family the following summer, as they were planning a trip to Uganda.

I was excited when the book arrived, *A Distant Grief.* The story of this young pastor, and his flight from Uganda with wife and young children, truly inspired me. I wanted to go to Uganda myself and meet him.

After much prayer and communication with Stephen DeMoss, my husband and I decided we would accept the invitation to join the DeMoss family on their mission trip to Uganda in 2012. The team would consist of a couple of nurses and my husband who, being a pharmacist, would set up some small clinics in a couple of villages while we were there.

I had seen heart-wrenching family situations doing ministry in Costa Rica. But my first experience in Uganda broke my heart. When we returned after our two-week trip, I sought out wise counsel because I had a hard time processing the pain I had seen with the orphans, the poverty, the young mothers trying to care for their children, and the lack of basic resources like water, electricity, food, clothing, and safe living conditions.

I felt called by the Holy Spirit to join the missionary work that Stephen Demoss had established through "Word in Deed Ministries," and was invited to join their Board of Directors in 2013. After hearing Reverend Sempangi speak, God placed in my heart His vision of ten churches, ten villages, ten schools, and ten clinics. Pastor Kefa had persuaded us that these remote villages needed not only the light of Jesus through the Gospel message, but also the basics of education and healthcare. This is the philosophy that when people see you care about their human needs they are more willing to listen to you talk about their spiritual needs.

This missionary caught what Stephen DeMoss had --- the love of the Ugandan people, and a heart to serve those less fortunate than myself. The past twelve years have been amazing and challenging, but I believe God now uses me as a contagious missionary too. I feel humbled and blessed to be part of a work that has served these villages in the Mukono district through medical missions, the building of churches and schools, a scholarship program, and developing a five-acre parcel of land to be a Community Resource Center.

This Resource Center is a work in progress, having just established a missionary home for visitors to stay in while they serve in the community. I have been blessed to help support the construction of a small church, from the first bricks being formed, to the installation of floors and laying on of a roof. Worshiping in that new building is so spiritually uplifting for me.

God's plans are always better than our own. I have learned so much about human nature, about trusting in God, about being patient while waiting for answers to prayer, about walking by faith and not sight.

I also say, with a small amount of pride, that we (through the generosity of others) have been able to enrich the lives of many children through the Scholarship Program. Many orphans have received support and tutoring for ten to twelve years, while growing in Christ through their education. Some have graduated from university. God has transformed many lives, especially mine, through the "contagious missionaries" that have crossed my path.

Today, May 2024, we prepare for what will be our 14th medical mission trip to Uganda. Back in 2017 a young man named Alec, just finishing high school (reminiscent of Stephen DeMoss), joined our mission trip along with his mother Jennifer. Alec was inspired during his first trip to become a doctor, and now, seven years later, will lead the medical team for the mobile clinics, having invited friends and professionals to join him this year. God took that young man's first experience to Uganda and transformed him into a servant of Christ with a medical degree. How amazing is that! Another "contagious" missionary.

Over the years I have prayed that some of the missionaries who have served with "Word in Deed Ministries" would continue to carry the torch and bring the light of Jesus into these communities for years to come. I would say God has answered this prayer for me.

Another persistent prayer is that "Word in Deed Ministries" will be able to keep serving these communities long after I am gone. There is a saying, "It takes a village," which is so true when it comes to serving God. I pray for the Ugandan people, whom I now call my friends. I pray for the children who now call me "Mama Lisa," that they will grow up to be warriors for Jesus and not tarnished by the historical corruption that is so prevalent in African countries. I pray that "Word in Deed Ministries" will retain strong leadership that will carry it forward. I pray for partnerships with other churches, schools, and individuals, to support the ministry so that it will not fade away or grow weary.

For as it says in Isaiah, "Even youths grow tired and weary, and young men stumble and fall; but those who hope in the Lord will renew their strength. They will soar on wings like eagles; they will run and not grow weary, they will walk and not be faint" (Isaiah 40:30, 31).

If you have been inspired by the stories in this book and want to become a "contagious missionary," I hope you will consider supporting "Word in Deed Ministries" so we can continue to live out the mission of James 1:27. Amen.

Credits

Special thanks to Pete Lytle: Invested many hours polishing my stories to a more readable form. He also played a significant hands-on role in clinics and "on the ground" in Uganda.

Gerald Mulindwa: First one to edit; longtime friend and encouragement to me for the work at hand.

Edward and Mary Kasaija: Mentored me over the years; hosted many teams in their home, and gladly shared resources with us weary travelers from abroad.

Kefa and Olivia Sempangi: Pastor and wife who secured a soldier for my house in the early days to protect the orphans and me from would-be thieves.

Jack and Rose Marie Miller: Courageous couple who pioneered our little exodus to a country in shambles, convinced of the need for salt and light in that part of the world. Rose Marie is turning 100 this year and still invested in writing the prelude to this book!

Linda Clemens: Spent countless hours editing, correcting, attaching Scriptures to many of the chapters. She and her husband Jack have sacrificed in many ways to bring hope to the "Pearl of Africa."

Theodora and Tessa DeMoss: Helped in numerous ways with the nuts and bolts of the book making sure certain things were consistent, punctuated properly and much more.

Sharon A. DeMoss, and Lisa Sorenson: Both women played significant roles as Presidents of "Word in Deed Ministries." Both labored tirelessly to keep the ministry alive for all these years. Lisa additionally wrote the postscript.

Barb Oelschlegel: Owner of the 'Purple Room (Chapter 34). Edited the book cover, regularly reviewed manuscript for typos, and also helped advise the author throughout the process of creating this writing.

My amazing Father and servant Mother (Robert and Dora DeMoss): Modeled servanthood–the genesis of any worthy principles conveyed in this book were learned at their knees and in their house.

Special Thanks to Andree Seu Peterson, Senior Writer World Magazine'. She consulted, advised and helped apply common sense adjustments for this my first manuscript.

There really are so many near and far who my mind goes to who spurred me on in this work. I am so grateful for each of you!

Note: All proceeds from this book will be given directly to the ministry in Uganda. Other donations would hugely help bring life back to these broken communities --- to cramped homes with no doors or windows and with mud floors where children sleep. Checks can be made out to: “Word in Deed Ministries.”

Correspondence is welcome! Email to:

Stephendemoss@hotelpaintersnetwork.com

Printed in the USA
CPSIA information can be obtained
at www.ICGtesting.com
LVHW082003041224
798129LV00009BC/1509
* 9 7 8 1 9 6 5 1 4 6 1 6 3 *